JUST WRITE THE DAMN BOOK

JUST WRITE THE DAMN BOOK

THE ENTREPRENEURS GUIDE TO WRITING AND PUBLISHING YOUR NON-FICTION BOOK

CHLOË BISSON

JUST WRITE THE DAMN BOOK

First Edition
ISBN: 978-1-7395671-1-8 Paperback

Published by Inspired By Publishing

The strategies in this book are presented primarily for enjoyment and educational purposes. Every effort has been made to trace copyright holders and obtain their permission for the use of copyright material.

The information and resources provided in this book are based upon the author's personal experience. Any outcome, income statements or other results, are based on the author's experience and there is no guarantee that your experience will be the same. There is an inherent risk in any business enterprise or activity and there is no guarantee that you will have similar results as the author as a result of reading this book.

The author reserves the right to make changes and assumes no responsibility or liability whatsoever on behalf of any purchaser or reader of these materials.

This book also comes with complimentary resources that guide you through how to write and publish your book. Get access to your resources here: www.chloebisson.com/justwrite

ACKNOWLEDGEMENTS

I would like to start by sharing my gratitude to the individuals who have made this book a reality.

To our incredible team at Inspired By Publishing, your passion for books and dedication to our authors has been instrumental in bringing this book to life.

Your creativity, curiosity and tireless efforts have set the stage for our writing and publishing services that became the foundations of this book and I am incredibly grateful for your support.

To the authors that we've published, your belief and trust in us to support you in your publishing journey was the spark of inspiration that led to this book.

It has been an honour to work with each of you, and I am thankful for you giving us the opportunity to perfect the book writing and publishing process with you.

TABLE OF CONTENTS

INTRODUCTION

Maybe right now you're reading this because you want to write a book.

Perhaps you know that writing a book will help your business to grow but you're not sure of what steps to take or where to start.

Or maybe right now you've already started writing your book but you don't know how to publish it.

Perhaps you've heard of people talking about self-publishing books and now you're wondering how to publish your book and get it into the hands of the people you want to work with.

Or possibly right now you've already published your book but it's currently sat on Amazon with little to no sales trickling in and you're wondering how others have launched bestselling books, not to mention if you're ever going to get the return on all of the blood, sweat and tears you put in to write it.

If any of those sound like you, then I'm really glad you've picked up this book.

In fact, if you're in the third category, then I'm sorry that this book wasn't there to help you earlier in your journey.

The good news is that by reading this book you're going to learn everything you need to write and publish your inspiring book.

But I have to be honest with you.

If you're reading this to learn how to publish your book fast so that you can get rich, make money while you sleep and get paid with "passive income" then this book *isn't* for you.

If you're looking for a book that will show you how to hack the Amazon algorithm and become a fake bestselling author with a garage full of your own books, then this book *isn't* for you.

But if you want a book that will show you the exact steps to write and publish your book so you can inspire others, share your knowledge and be known as the authority in your industry, then this book *is* for you.

Becoming a published author creates a level of authority. Whether it's your potential clients, friends or family, people will look at you differently when you publish your own books because there is a perception that someone who has published a book is an expert and authority on that subject.

Books have been a part of our daily lives since ancient times.

They have been used for telling stories, recording history and sharing information about our world. Although the ways that books are made have evolved over time, whether handwritten, printed on pages, or digitised online, their need remains timeless.

The first printed book was in 869 AD and since then books have developed into incredible tools for sharing knowledge, telling stories and leaving a legacy.

When I published my first book in 2019, I didn't really know what I was hoping to get from it or how to do it, all I knew was that I'd set myself a goal of writing a book and I wanted to do it to get my name out there and be seen as an expert in my industry.

Back then I was mentoring female entrepreneurs to start their own businesses and I'd started being invited to share my methods on stages and at live events to hundreds of women and one person asked me from the audience:

"Chloë, when are you going to write a book?"

The idea had come up before but I kept pushing it away with excuses like "I'm too busy", "I've got too many clients" and many other statements that I now know were helping me to procrastinate on writing and sharing my story.

But this time it felt different. This time something came over me and I thought:

"F*ck it! Yes I'll do it"

And before I knew it, I'd started my journey of becoming a published author. I knew how tempting it would be to let the procrastination kick back in so I'd set myself a goal of writing the book within 3 months. But as soon as I started writing it, it was like a tap turned on and I couldn't stop.

I wrote the book within 10 days and published it within 28 days.

I took everything I knew about marketing from my business and applied it to launching the book. Little did I know what was about to happen.

Determined and Dangerous launched on 2nd July 2019 and became a number 1 bestselling book in 11 categories on Amazon in just four hours.

It blew my mind and from that moment on, I was hooked. I fell in love with writing and publishing books. For me, it was less about the technical process and more about the personal journey I went on.

The release I felt writing my own story was amazing, the sense of fulfilment sharing my advice and knowledge, the feeling of satisfaction seeing it out in the world and the recognition I felt when people actually bought it!

It was a rollercoaster ride and I didn't really want to get off!

But what happened next was way more interesting… a friend reached out to me to ask how I did it and if I could help her do the same thing.

That was the start of Inspired By Publishing.

At the time of publishing this book we've published 35 bestselling books and helped 76 entrepreneurs write and publish their stories in books.

When starting this journey if you'd have asked me if I'm a writer, I would have said no. In fact, I would still say no now.

I'm not a writer. I'm a marketer.

Will you find a mistake or two in this book?

Probably.

But what I've learned from writing, reviewing and publishing many books is that there are clear steps to follow to write and publish a bestselling book.

Over the past few years I reflected on what really worked and the steps to take to ensure we continue to get results for our clients and so I created the Book Writing Blueprint™.

The Book Writing Blueprint™ is a six-step process that we use at Inspired By Publishing which takes you from having an idea for your book to getting your book in front of potential readers and all of the steps in between.

In this book I'm going to take you through each step of the Book Writing Blueprint™ in detail but for now, let's take a look at what the six steps are.

Purpose

The first step in the Book Writing Blueprint™ is getting clear on the purpose of publishing a book.

The majority of entrepreneurs start writing their books and never finish them, usually because life took over, they got too busy or they just lost interest.

All of those come back to the same issue which is not having a clear purpose for writing your book so we're going to get clear why you want to write your book and how it fits into your current business.

Promise

As the saying goes - if you speak to everyone then you'll help no one.

In book writing terms, this means that if we try to write a book that's generic enough to speak to everyone, it won't be specific enough to actually help anyone.

So we're going to map out who you want to actually read your book, your avatar, and what outcomes they'll get from reading it.

Plan

Writing a book is not a small project and it can feel like a mountain of a task when you look at a blank piece of paper so we're going to plan your book outline and structure so you know exactly where to start.

We're going to go through what content should and shouldn't go in, what knowledge you want to share and what advice you want to give so if you ever get writer's block or get stuck, you know where to go next.

Personalise

Your book might be written to help others but the true way to help others is by inspiring them with your own story.

In this step we'll be filtering through your stories so you know which parts to share in your book and how to tell them with impact and influence to really help your readers take action and believe they can do it too.

Prepare

Whether it's physically on paper or on a screen, most people get stuck when writing their book and find themselves overthinking, procrastinating and never actually finishing their manuscript.

So once you've got your content planned and your stories ready, we're going to run through how to pull it all together, let go of perfection and get your words written quickly and easily.

Publish

Now this step sounds extremely obvious but this is where a lot of entrepreneurs go very, very wrong. If you don't get this step right, you'll end up with a really well written book that becomes the world's best kept secret which clearly we don't want.

We're going to run through the key considerations when publishing your book and how to get your book into the hands or devices of people that need to read it.

As you can tell, there's a lot that we're going to cover in this book and how you use it is totally up to you.

You can follow the process step by step, or if there's specific parts you need help with straight away, you can jump to different chapters as you need to.

Finally, I know that writing a book can seem like a daunting task, but when you follow the steps in the Book Writing Blueprint™ it will, for sure, be an incredibly rewarding experience.

Not only will you have written and published your own book with your name on it that you can actually hold in your hands but imagine being at an event or speaking on stage and people asking you to sign your book and telling you how much it changed their lives.

Imagine seeing your business grow with new clients knowing who you are, reading your book and wanting to work with you.

That's what makes this journey worth it!

To help you on the journey, I've created additional resources for you to download and use as we go through the steps in the book.

You can access the additional resources area at www.chloebisson.com/justwrite.

There is no better feeling for an author than seeing your own published book in someone else's hands.

1
Purpose
2
Promise
3
Plan
4
Personalise
5
Prepare
6
Publish
Book Writing
Blueprint™

"If you want to change the world, pick up your pen and write."

- Martin Luther

1

WRITE A BOOK THAT CHANGES LIVES

So, here's a question for you: Why do you want to write a book?

The fact you're reading this book tells me that you already know that you want to write a book, but why?

Maybe you're a coach, trainer or speaker and you want to be seen as an authority in your industry.

Maybe you're an expert in a particular topic and you've got a message that you want to share with others.

Maybe you want to make an impact on the world and leave a legacy through writing your book.

In reality, writing your own non-fiction book is a tool that will help you achieve all of these but before writing your book, it's key to tune into why you're really doing this.

In the words of Simon Sinek:

"It's not what you do, but why you do it that really matters."

Most entrepreneurs that start writing a book focus too heavily on what they're writing and not why they're writing it and generally this leads to generic or uninspiring content.

So instead, we focus on getting clear on your why and using that in both the writing and marketing of your book.

When I wrote my first book, Determined and Dangerous, I was coaching and mentoring female entrepreneurs to leave the corporate world and start their own business and it was going really well!

I had some great clients and really enjoyed my lifestyle but I felt like I wasn't being 100% authentic with my audience.

When sharing my story with potential clients I had shared my experience of being made redundant from my job and using that fuel to start my own business which they could relate with.

But what I hadn't shared was what led to being made redundant and what really created the fire within me to start my own business.

I'd been diagnosed with severe clinical depression when I was 24 which led to me being signed off and unable to work for six months.

I went on a huge emotional rollercoaster and a life changing journey to say the least and when I got back into the corporate world, a lot had changed and I was made redundant.

So, the reason why I decided to write Determined and Dangerous was to share my expertise of overcoming professional challenges and starting my own business whilst also sharing more of my personal challenges that led me on that journey.

I'd hoped this would help potential clients to know, like and trust me more whilst also building my authority as an expert in my industry and that's exactly what happened.

Having a clear "why" will not only help you to work out what to include and not include in your book but it will also help you to create a stronger connection with your readers.

When readers can clearly understand your purpose for writing the book, they are more likely to feel invested in the content, connect with you on a deeper level and feel inspired to join you on the journey.

So, if you haven't already, ask yourself these questions:

Why do I want to write a book?

What is the bigger purpose of writing the book?

What has inspired me to write it?

Once you've got an idea on why you want to write your book, the next step is to get clear on how and where it fits into your business.

Now you might be writing a book because you want to give back, help others and leave a legacy and trust me, I get it.

That's exactly what drives me too.

But we've also got to be smart and strategic about how we do that.

I meet a lot of people who want to write their book so they have something to give to others for free and they say it's an "expensive business card".

Let me be clear. Your book is NOT an expensive business card.

How many times have you given someone a business card and they've replied with:

"Wow thank you so much, that was so valuable"

"I learnt so much by reading your business card"

"Reading your business card changed my life"

Okay, a little extreme, but you get the picture.

Books change people's lives.

Not business cards.

It's really that simple.

A book is a tool that can really inspire and influence the people that read it so don't devalue it.

I'm not saying that you can't give it to people for free, you absolutely can, but don't treat it like a business card.

If you want to give it to people for free then give it to people that actually need it and would value it.

Just Takeaways:

- **Discover Your Motivation:** Before you dive into writing your non-fiction book, take a moment to understand why you're doing it. Your "why" will shape not only your book's content but also how you promote it.

- **Learn from Simon Sinek:** Remember Simon Sinek's famous words – it's not just about what you do, but why you do it. Instead of fixating on what your book will cover, focus on the deeper reason driving you.

- **Be Authentic:** Share your why in the book and include personal stories and challenges. This honesty helps you build trust and authority with your audience.

- **Build Stronger Connections:** Your "why" isn't just about you; it's about your readers too. When your purpose shines through, your audience is more likely to connect with your work on a personal level.

- **Ask Yourself Key Questions:** Reflect on why you want to write this book, what larger goal it serves, and what fires up your passion to write it.

- **Strategise Your Book's Role:** While you may want to give back and leave a legacy, think strategically about how your book fits into your overall business plan.

- **Value Your Book:** Your book isn't just an expensive business card. It holds the power to genuinely impact lives and inspire readers.

- **Recognise Its Potential:** Books have the remarkable ability to change lives and ignite inspiration. Don't underestimate the profound impact your book can have.

- **Consider Your Audience:** If you decide to give your book away for free, ensure that it goes to individuals who genuinely need and appreciate it. Don't give it to just anyone who will take it.

Just Start Writing:

Get a blank piece of paper and answer each of the following questions:

- Why do I want to write a book?
- What's one thing I'd love to achieve by writing my book?
- How will my book help others?
- How will my book fit into my business?
- How will I monetise my book?
- How will I measure its success?
- What qualifies me to write it?

Bonus Hack: Once you've got clear on your "why", write it somewhere that you can see it!

Let it be a reminder that will help you stay focused and motivated throughout the writing process.

Writing a book is a significant task that can require a lot of time, effort, and energy and so the likelihood of you losing momentum at some point in the journey is pretty high.

Having a clear sense of purpose and "the why" for your book will help you to stay committed and focused, even when you don't feel like writing at all.

2

WHAT'S YOUR BOOK LEGACY?

When writing a book, it's vital to get really clear on what type of book you want to write and what topic you'd like to write about.

Within this book I'll be teaching you the process for non-fiction books based on real life events, people, or information.

They are great types of books for entrepreneurs to write because they can help your potential clients whilst elevating your status in your industry. Here are a few of the most common types of non-fiction books written by entrepreneurs:

Biographies and autobiographies

These are books that tell the story of your life, either from your own perspective or as written by someone else.

These books can work great if you have a big personal brand or celebrity status but if not, you've got to ask yourself, will people who don't know me want to read it?

Informative books

These are books that are informative and often teach a particular subject or topic, also known as "expert" books. These books work really well for showcasing your expertise, elevating your status and building your authority as an expert in your industry.

Self-help and personal development books

These are books that offer practical advice and guidance for personal development, self-improvement and wellbeing. These books can be great for entrepreneurs in the personal development industry as a method to help many people whilst building their authority.

Cookbooks

These are books that focus on recipes and cooking methods. These books can be great if the food or catering industry is relevant to your business.

If not, it's important to make sure there's a clear connection between the cookbook and the products or services that you offer.

Travel books

These are books that provide information about various destinations, including cultural information, historical sites, and practical advice for travel.

These books are great if you're in the travel industry as a tool to showcase your expertise on a particular location or area.

As you can probably tell, each type of book has its pros and cons so it's best to choose the type of book that relates the most to:

- Your business and the industry you work in
- Your avatar and what they would like to read
- Your expertise and where you'd like to showcase your authority

If you're still not sure which type of book you'd like to write when you first read the list, here's a quick tip.

Ask yourself:

What type of book am I most interested in reading?

What type of book would I have read early in my journey?

What type of book will help my audience the most?

In reality, our audience, our followers and our clients tend to be like us. That's how most marketing works so if you'd be interested in reading it, chances are they will too!

Now something you may not know about me is that my parents divorced when I was 10 years old. As an only child with parents that didn't talk for 11 years after their divorce, it was difficult to say the least.

When I wrote Determined and Dangerous I vaguely mentioned it but I didn't want it to turn into a book about divorce because that didn't align with my mission or vision for my business.

But the same couldn't be said for Caroline Martins. Since Caroline was 11 years old, she's wanted to help children whose parents were going through divorce.

By the time Caroline was 14 years old she'd written a self-help book helping children process their thoughts and emotions from their parents' divorce and her Mum, Eva, came to me to help get it in front of the children that needed it.

Caroline's book, "How do you survive when Mum and Dad separate?" launched on 29th April 2022 and has helped hundreds of children whose parents are going through separation or divorce.

Caroline's purpose for writing this book stemmed from her own experience of her parents' divorce when she learned that there was not enough support for children, not the type of support that she knew they needed.

This is why it's vital to write a book that considers your experience, your expertise and the person you want to help.

Now let's move onto the topic of your book.

A lot of entrepreneurs start writing books and then never finish them because they try to write about too many different topics.

My advice is one book = one topic.

For example, this book's topic is writing and publishing your book.

Could I also have shared tips about how to monetise your book?

Yes.

Could I also have shared tips about how to get your book featured in the media?

Yes.

Could I also have shared tips about how to turn your book into an audio book or online course?

Yes.

However, the reason why I haven't is because if you try to cover too many topics in your book, not only will it make it hard to explain to others but it will also mean you have to keep the content vague which means you won't be able to really help them.

It's better to select one key topic and give more detail in this one topic than trying to cover many different topics and only scratch the surface.

They don't want everything you know. They want the <u>one thing</u> you know that they need.

For example, in the book "The 7 Habits of Highly Effective People" by Stephen Covey, the key topic is on being more effective. Stephen Covey also has other books such as “The Speed of Trust” and “The Leader In Me” which all have different topics.

This means that having one key topic per book can give you more room for additional books in the future, which can allow you to attract more clients with slightly different or more specific challenges or problems.

For now though, remember that your book is a tool you’re using to share your expertise, help others and give your readers what they need.

The best way to achieve that is to focus on one key topic and provide them with all the knowledge they need in that key area.

But how do you know if people will actually want to read it?

There are millions of books published all around the world, so it’s safe to say that there will be at least one book with the same topic as yours, which is a good thing!

It means that there is an appetite for that topic.

Plus looking up similar books can give you something to research, review and model.

Many entrepreneurs start writing their books based on what their passions are, what their audience needs and so on but they forget to get their head out of their notes and have a look at what else is out there.

So, start your research as early as possible and have a look at what books are available that are similar to your ideas.

Go onto Google, search for books in your industry and have a look at what comes up. If you know of key experts in your industry, search for their names and see what you can find.

You may also be aware of some books that are not in your industry but you liked how they were written, how they were structured or how they came across.

This is also great to research so you can have a think about any particular books you'd like to model.

Make as many notes as possible and be specific about what you found, what you liked about the books you found and what you didn't like.

Keep track of the information you've gathered and organise it in a way that makes sense to you.

This will make it easier to reference when you start writing your book.

Just Takeaways:

- **Choose Your Book Type:** Take a minute to figure out what kind of book you want to create and what topic you want to explore. For entrepreneurs, non-fiction books or "expert" books are great to share your knowledge and experience.

- **Think About Your Audience:** To pick the right book type, put yourself in your readers' shoes. Ask yourself what kind of book you would have found helpful during your journey and what would genuinely benefit your audience. Remember, your readers are often a lot like you.

- **Write with Purpose:** Your book needs to have a clear mission and resonate with your own experiences, knowledge and the people you want to help.

- **One Book, One Topic:** Focus on one main topic when you're writing your book. Specialising in one subject allows you to dive deep and give the most value to your reader.

- **Do Your Research:** Before you get into writing, make sure there's a demand for your chosen topic by looking into similar books in your field. Explore works by experts and even consider books from unrelated areas if you like their style or structure. Jot down what you liked and didn't like.

Just Start Writing:

Grab a pen and answer each of the following questions:

What book do I want to write?

What would I love to write about?

What stories or experiences would I love to share?

What type of book would make the most sense for my business?

What type of book would relate best to my industry?

What type of book would my avatar want to read?

What type of book would showcase my expertise the best?

What topics could I write about?

Which topic am I most passionate about?

Which topic would my audience benefit from the most?

What other experts or celebrities in my industry have written books on this topic?

What other books are available on this topic?

What books would I like to model?

What did I specifically like about them?

If you're like me and you like to journal out your ideas, there's a "Book Ideas Journal" in the additional resources area which has the questions from Chapter 1 and Chapter 2.

You can download the "Book Ideas Journal" at www.chloebisson.com/justwrite.

6
Publish
1
Purpose
5
Prepare
Book Writing
Blueprint™
2
Promise
4
Personalise
3
Plan

"Making promises and keeping them is a great way to build a brand"

- Seth Godin

3

ATTRACT THE PERFECT READER

Now that you know the type and topic for your book, it's time for us to figure out who we want to actually read it.

Spoiler alert: Your book is not about you. It's about your reader!

If you've spent time on your marketing before, this may be a nice refresher for you (with a bit of a twist!)

Getting clear on who you want your reader to be before starting to write your book means that you can tailor your writing to their needs, wants and interests, and increase the likelihood that they'll actually find your book valuable and relevant.

It also means you can create content that speaks directly to them and build a stronger connection, which ultimately makes it easier for you to sell your book.

For example, let's say you're writing a book about personal growth and self-development. Whilst this is a very clear industry and book genre, there are so many different types of readers.

One type of reader might be someone who is in their mid-20s and feeling a little lost in their life. They're looking for guidance and direction, and they want to figure out what their life purpose is.

If you were writing a book for this particular reader, you'd probably want to share more practical tips and exercises that they can do to help them get started and find their direction.

On the other hand, another type of reader could be someone who is in their 40s or 50s and is feeling a bit stuck. They've been working in the same job for years and they're feeling unfulfilled and unchallenged.

If you were writing this book, you may give them strategies to reignite their passion and figure out how to make a change. This type of reader may benefit greater from more in-depth, philosophical insights and ideas.

Whilst you could argue that you may teach both readers the same principles, the way you write and the examples that you'll use in the book would differ a lot due to the nature of the reader.

Now let's deal with the elephant in the room.

Many entrepreneurs don't focus on one reader because they think that it will mean less people will read their book, but they couldn't be more wrong.

My perspective is that if you try to help everyone, you'll attract no one.

Just because you know who your book is for doesn't mean that other people won't read it too. If anything, the clearer you focus on your target reader, the more likely you'll get more readers because it will resonate better with those who it is meant for.

So, it's time to get crystal clear on who your book is actually for.

This might be really obvious to you if you're already running a business, because you might have an avatar quite clearly documented, however I did say there was a twist.

We're focusing on your reader and their specific needs when reading your book, so there are a few key things to keep in mind including:

Their demographic: age, gender, education, location, occupation, etc.

Their interests and hobbies: what does your reader enjoy doing in their free time?

Their pain points: what challenges or struggles is your reader facing right now?

Their goals and aspirations: what does your reader want to achieve in their life?

Their needs: what does your reader need to learn or do differently?

Considering these factors can help you get a clearer picture of who your reader is and what they want to get specifically from your book.

Once you've got the basics down, the next step is to get more specific about your reader in terms of books.

What kind of books do they read?

What kind of tone of voice do they respond to?

What kind of writing style do they like?

Would they prefer longer or shorter chapters?

Would they benefit from activities included in the book?

If you're not 100% sure or you feel like you're assuming, it's time to get your research hat back on and ask!

The best way I found to do this was to create a questionnaire asking these specific questions.

Another option which is slightly more time consuming but could get you better answers is conducting interviews with a few of your current clients that you feel would be great examples of your reader.

Whichever research strategy you choose, it will help you gather more information about their reading habits, interests and preferences, while also getting them curious about the book that you're writing!

We've already covered the fact that your book is less about you and more about your reader so it's probably not a surprise that we need to adapt to what works best for our reader, even if it's not our natural preference!

Once you know your reader better, it will help you make decisions about things like the tone of voice you use in your book, the length of your chapters, and the overall structure of your book, which we will cover in later chapters.

Authors pave a path for their readers to follow. You need to know your reader so you can pave the path they need.

Just Takeaways:

- **Focus on Your Reader:** Your book isn't about you; it's all about your reader. Keep their interests front and centre as you write.

- **Tailor Your Content:** Personalise your writing to meet your reader's needs, wants, challenges and interests. This connection will boost your book's value and sales.

- **Demographics Matter:** Consider your reader's age, gender, education, location and occupation to understand their perspective and preferences.

- **Align With Their Goals:** Understand their life goals and aspirations to provide guidance that resonates with their ambitions.

- **Meet Their Needs:** Figure out what your reader needs to learn or change in their life and make sure your book provides practical insights.

- **Learn Their Reading Habits:** Investigate what kinds of books your ideal reader usually reads, their preferred tone and writing style to align with their preferences.

- **Adapt Your Tone:** Adjust your writing style to match the tone that your reader responds to best, creating a more personal connection.

- **Structure For Their Comfort:** Consider whether your reader prefers longer or shorter chapters and structure your book accordingly for a smoother reading experience.

Just Start Writing:

Create a survey or short questionnaire and send it to your audience asking for feedback.

Interview a handful of current clients or contacts that you feel would be a good example of your reader.

Collate the results and create an avatar of your reader.

We have a "Reader Avatar" template that we use for all of our books to ensure we've captured the information we need on our readers.

You can download this template in the resources area at www.chloebisson.com/justwrite.

4

THE #1 WAY TO MAKE YOUR BOOK STAND OUT

After publishing over 35 books with Inspired By Publishing, I noticed that when I met each new author I kept asking one simple question:

"What's your big promise?"

Many of them looked at me blankly, and then I realised that this comes back to my expertise as a marketer first, author second.

In marketing terms, a "big promise" is a bold and compelling statement about your book that explains a significant benefit or outcome that your readers will get when reading your book.

The goal of your big promise is to capture the attention and interest of potential readers, to create a sense of excitement and anticipation, and to differentiate it from other books in the same industry.

So, putting it simply, your big promise is the number one thing that your readers will gain after reading your book.

For example, if you're writing a book to help someone go through a break up, the big promise may be to be confident, happy and proud to be single.

If you're writing a book on healthy eating, the big promise could be to live a healthier lifestyle and be full of energy every morning.

Your big promise will not only help you write a better book but it will also help you sell it.

My big promise for you is that, after reading this book, you'll have written and published your own book.

And the biggest difference between books that sell and books that don't is that the books that don't are missing a clear big promise. If people don't know what outcome they're going to get, they are not going to buy it.

Your big promise is a reason for you to write and a reason for them to buy.

You want your big promise to make your book stand out and show people why reading your book isn't just a nice thing to buy, it's a must-have.

For example, if you teach business owners how to use Google to get customers then how about a big promise to show them how to do it specifically using Google Ads.

That's exactly what Ajay Dhunna did with his bestselling book in 2022. Ajay is a marketer that specialises in all things Google and had already written the majority of his book and came to me to publish it.

Marketing on Google being such a large topic, it was key for Ajay to have a really clear big promise to make his book stand out.

Ajay decided to promote his book as the book that helps business owners win customers from google ads and this became his big promise.

We launched Ajay's book, "How To Win Customers With Google Ads", on 10th November 2022 and, because of Ajay's clear big promise, he made over £10,000 in less than a week after his book launch, from clients who wanted to work with him, even before they'd even read the content of his book.

This is the power of the big promise.

The reason this big promise worked so well for Ajay was because it was specialised and niched.

It wasn't a full manual on how to learn everything on google ads, it didn't teach all aspects of Google from SEO to Ads, it also didn't teach other marketers how to use google ads for their clients. It was specifically about winning more customers from Google Ads; one ideal reader, one topic and one big promise.

To work out your big promise, here are some steps that you can take:

1. **Get clear on your reader**

If you haven't already got clarity on who your book is intended for from Chapter 3, now is the time to do it so that you can determine what kind of big promise would appeal to them based on their problems and goals.

2. **Identify the main benefits of your book**

Think about the benefits your readers will gain from reading your book. What will they learn? What will they be able to do after reading it? How will their lives be improved?

3. Choose a compelling big promise

Based on the benefits you've identified, craft a statement that summarises the big promise of your book.

Make it clear, concise and compelling.

Your big promise should inspire readers to want to learn more about your book and the benefits it offers.

So, with that all in mind, what is your big promise?

What's the one thing that you want your readers to leave with after reading your book?

Remember, people aren't reading your book to learn a process or a skill. They are reading your book because they want to leave with an outcome.

Now with great power comes great responsibility. Yes, I did just quote Spider-Man.

Seriously though, it's important to note that making a big promise also comes with a level of responsibility.

Your big promise needs to be authentic and achievable, because your readers will be expecting you to deliver.

Just Takeaways:

- **The Power of a Big Promise:** In the world of book publishing, having a clear and compelling "big promise" is essential. Your big promise is a bold statement about the significant benefit or outcome your readers will gain from your book.

- **Capture Readers' Attention:** Your big promise is a tool to capture the attention and interest of potential readers. It sets your book apart from others in the same genre and creates excitement and anticipation.

- **Impact on Sales:** A well-defined big promise not only improves your book's content but also aids in its sales. Readers are more likely to buy a book when they know what outcome they can expect.

- **Steps to Determine Your Big Promise:** To craft your big promise, follow these steps: 1) Clarify your target audience, 2) Identify the main benefits of your book and 3) Craft a compelling and concise statement that summarises your big promise.

- **Readers Seek Outcomes:** Readers pick up your book not just to acquire knowledge but to achieve specific outcomes. Your big promise should align with these expectations.

- **Do What You Say You Will:** A big promise must be authentic and achievable. Readers will hold you accountable for delivering on your promise, so exercise this power responsibly.

Just Start Writing:

Fill in the blank:

By reading my book my readers will be able to

____

____

Make a note of your big promise as you're writing your book.

Keep reflecting back to it as you write, ensuring the book delivers on the promise.

Book Writing Blueprint™
1
Purpose
2
Promise
3
Plan
4
Personalise
5
Prepare
6
Publish

"There are dreamers and there are planners; the planners make their dreams come true"

- Edwin Louis Cole

5

FIND YOUR SECRET SAUCE

Every book takes a reader on a journey.

Before writing your book, it's important to get clear where the journey starts and finishes.

Now, for full disclosure, there are many different ways to write a non-fiction book. Most non-fiction books are written in one of two ways:

Story-based: This leads with a biography or story of how the author has achieved something and includes lessons or processes along the way. This is the way most celebrities or famous authors write their books.

Process-based: This leads with a process or strategy of how to achieve something and includes personal stories and experiences to explain the points.

This is the way most entrepreneurs write their books.

The biggest difference is whether you lead with your story or with your process.

If you are already considered a celebrity and have a significant following that would be interested in hearing your story, then story-based could be a great route.

However, for most entrepreneurs, this isn't the case.

If entrepreneurs without celebrity status write a story-based book, they'll be great at getting their first few readers, who are usually their clients and loved ones.

But the reach of their book will tend to dry up because there's no consistent flow of people interested in learning more about their story.

I promised you that I'd be honest and authentic in this book and so here we go.

I learned this the hard way when I wrote Determined and Dangerous because I wrote it as a story-based "how to" book.

Despite the goal being to help others, the process was taught based on telling my story and therefore when potential readers came across the book, unless they

People start reading because of them but they continue reading because of you.

knew me well enough, there wasn't a big enough pull for them to read it.

The question you need to ask yourself is "would someone who doesn't know me yet, want to read this book?".

The harsh reality is that for most entrepreneurs who don't have a big brand or status, the answer is usually no.

This is why the best way to write your book is process-based as even though the readers don't need to know you yet, they still have a problem that your book can fix. Once they're reading the book and learning the process, they buy into you and become loyal followers, fans and even clients.

The process-based approach is fairly straightforward to map out as it simply teaches your reader the process to get from A to B, with A representing where your book starts and B representing where your book finishes.

A is where your reader is starting their journey with you.

This is where they may be facing problems, challenges and doubts. This is known as the "Before".

B, however, is quite the opposite. This is where your reader wants to be, where they have achieved results and outcomes. This is known as the "After".

Every book has an A and a B.

By defining the A and the B, it helps us to map out the outline of our book based on the journey in between the two points.

For example, if we use the famous book "Rich Dad, Poor Dad" by Robert Kiyosaki, it takes the reader on a journey to achieve financial freedom.

It starts with not having any financial assets and throughout the book, Robert Kiyosaki teaches the reader to understand money, the framework to achieve financial freedom and he shares what he learnt from his "Rich Dad".

Starting with A, consider what your reader may be experiencing right now before they read your book:

- Problems
- Challenges
- Struggles
- Paint points
- Negative feelings
- Doubts

You might find that you have a few that "it could be this or it could be that" – don't worry about the "ifs" or "buts", and if you have a couple of different scenarios, include them both for now.

With B, it's a very similar process when focusing on where they want to be after reading your book:

- Goals
- Outcomes
- Emotions
- Positive results

Be as specific as possible so you can start to get ideas of how to get them there.

By writing the lists for the before and the after for your book, not only will you have a clear journey for your book to take the reader on but, when we come to marketing your book, you've already done most of the hard work!

When you know A and B, then it's time to create your book outline; the list of the steps you're going to teach them on how they can go from A to B and ultimately achieve the big promise.

Now if you're a logical, process-oriented person, you're going to love this next part.

If, however, the thought of having a strict step-by-step process is painful and you prefer to let things flow, then we can make this work for you too.

The process that takes your readers from A to B can be a simple straightforward set of steps like:

A: Step 1 → Step 2 → Step 3 → Step 4 → B

And it can also be more free-flowing in the style of specific tips or lessons that don't have to be in a set order like:

A: Lesson 1 → Tip 2 → Tip 3 → Lesson 4 → B

There's no perfect way to structure your book outline.

What makes it perfect is the fact that it takes your reader from A to B.

Here's some guidance on how to create your book outline:

Step 1) Brainstorm the main points

Write down all of the important points and ideas you want to include in your book.

Think about your reader going from A to B.

- What steps do they need to take?
- What processes should they follow?
- What strategies would you recommend?
- What advice would you give them?
- What lessons do they need to learn?

Keep it simple and don't add too much detail yet.

Just a few bullet points are all you need at this stage.

Step 2) Organise your points into a logical order

Determine the flow of information and arrange your main points in an order that you'd recommend.

This would typically be the order that most people would follow to go from A to B.

Are there specific steps or lessons that your reader will experience first?

Are there specific tips you'd save until later in the book?

Review the list you wrote in Step 1 and put them in an order that makes sense to take your reader from A to B.

Step 3) Review your outline

Read through your outline and make changes as necessary.

Make sure it makes sense and ask yourself:

"If they follow the steps in this order, will they get to B?".

If there is anything missing, add it to your list.

Having a book outline will help your book to stay focused on exactly what your reader needs and stop you going off on a tangent when you start writing!

Not to mention if your reader gets confused reading the book, they're never going to finish it.

Just Takeaways:

- **Story vs. Process:** Non-fiction books typically fall into two categories: story-based or process-based. The key distinction is whether you lead with your personal story or the process/strategy you want to teach.

- **Story-Based for Celebrities:** If you are a celebrity or have a significant following interested in your story, a story-based approach may work. However, this is the exception, not the rule.

- **Process-Based for Most Entrepreneurs:** For most entrepreneurs without a big brand or status, a process-based book is more effective. Readers are attracted by the promise of solving their problems, and they buy into you as they learn the process.

- **Start with Clarity:** Before embarking on your book-writing journey, define where it begins and ends. Every book has a starting point (A) where readers face challenges and an ending point (B) where they achieve goals and positive outcomes.

- **Make Marketing Easy:** Identifying where your reader is before and after they read your book makes marketing your book easier, as you've already defined the transformation your readers will experience.

- **Create Your Book Outline:** Knowing A and B will help you to outline the steps, lessons, key points or ideas that will guide your readers from A to B. The outline can be structured or free-flowing; what matters is the journey it offers.

Just Start Writing:

Follow the steps in the chapter and put the bullet points into a list, starting with A and ending with B:

A (BEFORE):

Chapter 1:

Chapter 2:

Chapter 3:

Chapter 4:

Chapter 5:

Chapter 6:

Chapter 7:

Chapter 8:

Chapter 9:

Chapter 10:

B (AFTER):

If you need more or less than 10 chapters, just add or remove them.

We've included a "Book Outline Template" in the additional resources area. You can download it at www.chloebisson.com/justwrite.

6

WHAT IF NO ONE READS IT

By now, you're probably feeling pretty motivated to start writing, but there's a vital thing to consider before you go any further.

What if no one wants to read your book?

Ouch.

I know, it's not a nice thing to think about but I'd rather you overcome that now before you start actually writing.

We've all had moments in our lives where we've had an idea for something really cool and exciting, but when it comes to launching it, we don't get the same response from the outside world.

It's painful enough if you've spent hours recording an online course and get no clients, but imagine spending months putting your heart and soul into a book only to find out you're the only reader!

There is nothing worse than writing a book that no one wants to read.

So, before you go any further, it's vital to get feedback on your idea.

There are a few different types of people you could ask for feedback:

Known and trusted contacts

These are friends, family members, or co-workers who you think would be interested in the topic of your book.

This is a great place to start your research because they already know you and likely value what you do, so they're the perfect audience to give you honest feedback and help you refine your concept.

Industry experts

These are experts in your field who can give you feedback on your concept. This could be someone with a specific qualification in the field or a seasoned professional with years of experience.

A great way to ask for feedback could be to ask if you could interview them for your book and, as you're sharing the concept, ask them for feedback.

This way you're getting great insights for your book whilst also vetting your ideas.

Publishers

If you're serious about getting results with your book, a great way to get feedback is to hire a publisher because they'll be equally as motivated by the success of your book as you are.

A good publisher will be able to give you feedback on your concept, refine your ideas and make sure you've got the best chance of publishing success.

When reaching out for feedback, the goal is to get useful, high quality feedback.

And I always say "the quality of the answer is defined by the quality of the question".

So, it's key to ask the high quality questions to get the high quality answers.

Here are a few prompts of questions to ask:

1. What are your initial thoughts?
2. What do you like the most?
3. What do you like the least?
4. What do you find most valuable?
5. What, if anything, is missing?
6. Would you buy this book? *(This is a great question if you're asking people who are your ideal reader!)*

Finally, there is no point in gathering feedback if we're not going to do something with it.

If you receive positive feedback then great news – keep going!

If, however, you don't receive the feedback you would have liked, then it's time to take a deeper look.

Review the feedback and consider:

- Were they the right people to ask?

- What areas specifically didn't they like?
- What would they have preferred instead?

There are lessons in everything so dig deeper and find out more about the sort of books they'd like to read and what changes you could make to your original idea.

You don't need to start again or get rid of all of your hard work – it's about adapting.

In the words of Ross from Friends: "PIVOT!"

Just Takeaways:

- **Crucial Consideration:** Don't wait until your book is published to find out if anyone wants to actually read it. Get some feedback on your book concept early in the game. You don't want to invest months of hard work into something that might not resonate with readers.

- **Get A Range Of Feedback:** When seeking feedback, you can start by asking friends, family, or co-workers who share an interest in your book's topic for their honest input. Reach out to industry experts for valuable insights, and don't overlook the potential benefits of working with publishers who can provide feedback and enhance your book's chances of success.

- **Ask The Right Questions:** When seeking feedback, the key is asking the right questions. Be curious and ask open questions to find out what they think, what they like and dislike and if they'd actually buy your book. Give them permission to be as honest as possible so you get valuable feedback that will really make a difference.

- **Taking Action On Feedback:** The act of getting feedback is only as valuable as the action taken from it. If the feedback is positive, keep going! If there's any valuable feedback to implement, pinpoint what needs changing and consider their feedback.

- **Adapt and Pivot:** When taking on board feedback, you don't need to start from scratch or discard your hard work. Feedback is a tool for fine-tuning, not starting over so take on board the feedback and adapt or pivot as needed to make your book the best it can be.

- **Thanks But No Thanks:** Not all feedback needs to be taken on board if you don't feel that it aligns with you. Assess whether you asked the right audience and give yourself permission to not use their feedback if necessary.

Just Start Writing:

Reach out to 3 people and get feedback on your book concept. Tell them about your ideas and ask them the six questions.

If possible, get the feedback either in person or on Zoom so that you can have a conversation about it rather than black and white text.

7

THE CONTENT QUADRANT™ EVERY CHAPTER NEEDS

"Fail to prepare, prepare to fail" is pretty accurate in most cases and writing your book is no different.

Most entrepreneurs start with a blank piece of paper when writing their books and then blame their lack of writing on "writer's block" when actually the only block is around the lack of planning.

Every time I've written chapters, whether in my books or in books that I've co-authored, I've always struggled to start with a blank page.

I'd find myself setting time aside to write and an hour later still be staring aimlessly at a blank page and achieving absolutely nothing.

What I found made the process so much easier was not starting with a blank page but instead starting with a plan, more specifically, a chapter plan.

Your chapter plan is an outline of content that you want to include in that chapter. You can make a note of explanations that you want to use, stories that you want to share and strategies that you want to teach – whatever you can think of!

I always recommend keeping it as a one-pager with bullet points of your ideas for that chapter.

Your chapter plan can also help you make sure you've included all of the important aspects in each chapter to help your reader understand the concepts better.

Remember, if you are writing a non-fiction "how to" book, you are teaching your reader how to do something and therefore you need to plan each chapter like you would plan a lesson.

I first came across this concept when I created my first online course and then went on to teach lots of entrepreneurs how to do the same in the 30 Day Course Creation Challenge.

When creating an online course, the goal is to teach the participants a particular skill or give them a piece of knowledge.

This means there are key aspects you need to include for the best possible chance that the person will, firstly, understand the material and, secondly, remember how and when to use it. And writing a non-fiction book is exactly the same.

The key difference to how I teach book writing is to have a balance of information and inspiration:

Information - The definitions, facts, figures and processes.

Inspiration - The meaning behind it, why it's important, your experiences and your story relevant to that topic.

After all, people are much more likely to remember what you teach them when you actually make them feel something.

The key elements are known as the Content Quadrant™:

Content Quadrant™

WHAT	WHY
HOW	WHO

<u>WHAT</u>

What is the topic?

What are they reading about in this chapter?
What definitions can you include?

<u>WHY</u>

Why do they need to read this?

Why is it relevant and important to them?

The Why is something that SO many entrepreneurs miss out on in their chapters.

Ultimately, if people don't know why they need to read it or why it's relevant to them, they either won't remember it or they won't read it at all.

HOW

How do they do it?

What is the process or strategy they can follow?

This is what I like to call "the good stuff".

It's what they need to do to fix the problems and it's usually the main reason people have bought your book in the first place.

WHO

Who has also had this experience?

Whose story or example can you share?

Who can they relate to?

This helps to build relatability into your book as it gives you the opportunity to share stories with your reader.

These can be stories of your own experience, case studies of your clients, stories of celebrities or famous people or even research studies which could back up your point.

Now let me take you through a theoretical example and you can fill in the blanks:

<u>WHAT</u>

In this chapter we're going to cover ________________

What do I mean by ________________*?*

By ________________ *I mean* ________________ *and* ________________ *can be defined by* ________________

That is a simple example of how you can structure the WHAT.

Now let's look at WHY

<u>WHY</u>

________________ *is so important when it comes to doing* ________________

In the situation where you're doing ________________ *then* ________________ *could happen and* ________________ *could go wrong.*

This is why it's so important when doing ________________ *that you consider* ________________

That's an example of how you include the WHY.

HOW

In order to achieve ________________ *there are* _____ *steps to follow.*

Step 1 ________________________________

Step 2 ________________________________

Step 3 ________________________________

You get the gist here.

Now let's look at the WHO.

WHO

This is what I learnt on my journey when I achieved ________________

I ________________ and now I've been able to ________________

That's if you want to include your own story and we're going to cover that in later chapters.

Now if you want to include someone else's story or a case study, this is how you could do it:

This is exactly what my client ________________ achieved when they did ________________ and this is what happened ________________.

Hopefully understanding that structure using a blank example can help to either literally fill in the blanks or just understand how it can flow and how it can work from one part of the Content Quadrant™ to the other.

Using the Content Quadrant™ in each chapter, you can ensure that your readers have all of the information they need to fix their problem and achieve the big promise.

But don't forget to add your own style into the mix!

You don't necessarily have to write each chapter in the order of the Content Quadrant™:

WHAT – WHY – HOW – WHO

Ideally, you want your chapters to read slightly different to each other so whilst your chapter plan may include all four pillars, it won't necessarily write it in that order.

Remember you're not a robot and you don't want your reader to feel that as they read your book!

If you're anything like me and you get stuck in your head quite easily, it can also be a good strategy to look externally for ideas.

After all, you don't know what you don't know, right?

Have a look into books, articles, and other resources that are related to your topic to get an idea of what information is already out there and what is missing.

There are lots of offline resources that you can explore too like attending local conferences and events in your industry.

This can be a great way to get some inspiration with different approaches and opinions you can use whilst building up your network!

People learn from you through information but they remember you through inspiration

Just Takeaways:

- **Start with A Plan:** Instead of struggling with a blank page, begin your writing process with a chapter plan. This plan outlines the content you want to include in each chapter, including explanations, stories and strategies.

- **Less Is More:** Keep your chapter plan concise, ideally as a one-page document with bullet points outlining your ideas for that chapter. This approach helps you stay organised and focused.

- **Put Your Teacher Hat On:** When writing a non-fiction "expert" book, approach each chapter as if you were planning a lesson. This perspective ensures that you'll explain the information effectively and help your reader to learn easily.

- **Information vs Inspiration:** Include both information and inspiration in your chapters. Engaging readers emotionally makes them more likely to remember and apply what you teach.

- **Content Quadrant™:** Use the Content Quadrant™ (What, Why, How and Who) to ensure that your reader understands the information they need to solve their problems and achieve the book's big promise.

- **Let It Flow:** While the Content Quadrant™ provides a structure, it's not necessary to write chapters in a rigid order. Allow your writing style to flow naturally, and avoid it sounding robotic.

- **Be Inspired By Others:** When you find it hard to come up with ideas or get stuck while writing, read other books, articles, or blogs related to your topic. These sources can give you new insights and ways of thinking that can make your book more interesting and informative.

Just Start Writing:

Pick a chapter from your book outline and create a one page chapter plan using the Content Quadrant™:

WHAT
WHY
HOW
WHO

Start with a chapter that you're most interested in or inspired by and write a few bullet points on what you'd like to include in the chapter using the list above.

If you'd like a template to fill in, download the template chapter plan in the resources area at www.chloebisson.com/justwrite.

6
Publish
1
Purpose
Book Writing
Blueprint™
5
Prepare
2
Promise
4
Personalise
3
Plan

"When you shut down vulnerability, you shut down opportunity"

- Brené Brown

8

THE 5FS TO BUILD A REAL CONNECTION

At some point when writing your book, if you haven't already, you'll hear a quiet voice in your head saying:

"Why would anyone read my book?".

Whether you're writing a book to help others, leave a legacy, get more clients or anything in between, getting readers to actually read your book is key.

It might sound obvious but there are millions of non-fiction books written by entrepreneurs just like us where the reader doesn't even finish reading the book.

This isn't because the book isn't valuable, it's because the author hasn't connected with the reader on a personal level and therefore the reader isn't engaged or motivated to continue reading.

In the last chapter we looked at the importance of getting the balance right between information and inspiration.

In this section of the book, we're focusing purely on the inspiration piece which tends to fit into the "Why" or "Who" parts of the Content Quadrant™:

WHY - A great way to show the importance of the topic or why something is needed is by sharing your own personal experience.

WHO - If you've experienced the process or topic that you're teaching in a chapter then you can use your own personal experience to emphasise the point that you're teaching.

The general rule when writing your book is that as you teach the process to take your reader from A to B, you can include a story, experience or metaphor to compliment the process and weave the personal stories throughout the book.

This way, every story has a point and every point has a story.

Now the stories have to be relevant to the journey that your book is taking your reader on.

Your book isn't about you but it must include you.

Unless your book is about pets or animals, losing your first pet at a young age is probably not a story that is relevant to your book.

You've got to think about your experiences that are relevant to your reader and the journey of your book.

They don't have to be exactly the same experiences, the key is that they have the same theme or topic.

For example, if I was writing a book about starting a business, then the story of when I started my first business would be extremely relevant as it's the exact same topic.

On the other hand, if I was writing about how to let go of a relationship, I could also share a story of when my ex-partner was unfaithful ending in us breaking up.

Whilst it's not exactly the same story, the feelings and theme of being let down and alone are the same.

There are lots of different types of stories and personal experiences you can include in your book.

The best way to ensure you're including the most impactful stories, you can follow the 5Fs:

- Firsts
- Fears
- Failures
- Frustrations
- Fortunes

Firsts:

Firsts are memorable experiences or events that happened to you for the very first time, such as a first job, first love, first travel experience or first success, for example.

Firsts are really powerful when teaching a process because they're often what your reader is about to experience or may even be experiencing right now which makes them extremely relatable and impactful.

Fears:

Fears are moments or situations within your journey where you felt scared, afraid or dread.

I know that can feel very exposing and uncomfortable but by sharing the fears that you experienced in various parts of your book it will help your reader connect with you on a deeper emotional level.

It will also help your reader to understand how you overcame that fear and how they can too, giving more value and support.

Failures:

Failures are exactly what it sounds like; share moments where you've failed.

Similar to the other Fs, sharing relevant failures with your reader brings in a refreshing vulnerability into your book whilst also showing your reader that you're not perfect, creating a stronger human connection.
When you include examples of where you've failed and how you bounced back, it helps to build your authority as to why you're the expert to show them how to overcome this failure or avoid it all together.

Frustrations:

The best way to tell a story in a book is by bringing in emotions and frustrations which many readers and writers can relate to.

Maybe when you were on the journey that you're taking your reader on, something didn't go to plan and it left you feeling frustrated or disappointed, this is what you want to include in your book.

By including your frustrations, it helps the reader to understand your experience, create empathy and build a stronger connection with you as the author.

Fortunes:

Fortunes are wins, results or successes that you've achieved on your journey, such as reaching a goal or overcoming an obstacle to achieve a positive outcome.

These are great ways to inspire, motivate and uplift your reader, as they show your determination, hard work and perseverance to achieve the end goal.

They can also build your credibility, as your fortunes are often what your reader wants to achieve from reading the book.

In an ideal world, you'd want to sprinkle a few of each type of personal experience within the chapters of your book to help create that personal connection throughout.

Just Takeaways:

- **Connection Is Key:** To make your book a success, connecting with your readers through sharing your personal expertise is vital. Many readers don't finish reading books because they don't connect with the author.

- **Share The Why:** Demonstrate the importance of your topic by sharing your personal experiences related to it. This helps readers understand why your message matters and why it's important for them.

- **Personal Expertise:** If you've been through what you're teaching, leverage your personal experience to emphasise your points to enhance your credibility and show your expertise.

- **The 5Fs For Impact:** For the most impactful stories, follow the 5Fs - Firsts, Fears, Failures, Frustrations, and Fortunes. These stories inspire, motivate, and uplift your readers while building rapport with you as the author.

- **Stories With Purpose:** As you guide your readers from point A to B, incorporate stories, experiences, or metaphors that are relevant to your book's journey. Focus on experiences that align with your reader's journey.

Just Start Writing:

Thinking about your personal experiences relevant to the topic of your book:

<u>Firsts:</u>

What were the first milestones that you hit?

What were the first wins or successes that you achieved?

What were the first challenges that you experienced?

<u>Fears:</u>

When you started your journey, what were you afraid of?

What doubts did you have?

When you were on the journey, what fears or doubts did you experience?

<u>Failures:</u>

What failures did you experience?

What mistakes did you make?

What was the impact of these mistakes or failures?

Frustrations:

When did you feel frustrated or disappointed?

What happened that made you feel frustrated?

Fortunes:

What wins, results or successes did you achieve?

What was the impact of these fortunes?

You can also map out your 5Fs using the "5Fs Story Framework" in the resources area. You can download it at www.chloebisson.com/justwrite.

9

HOW TO AUTHENTICALLY TELL YOUR STORY

This is the part where you can let your hair down and let your imagination take over.

The art of storytelling is the skilful and creative practice to convey a message, inspire or educate an audience.

It has been used for thousands of years to pass down knowledge, share experiences and preserve history.

The only difference is that, as you're writing a non-fiction book that teaches your reader to achieve an outcome, you don't want your book to feel like it's all about YOU so the art lies in telling your story in a way that helps your reader.

It goes beyond the traditional non-fiction books that present raw data or dry facts and instead, weaves in inspiring stories that capture your reader's attention and imagination.

No one wants to be an author that writes a book that people get bored of reading and just flick through the pages to skip the long winded waffle to get to the valuable parts.

So, the ultimate goal of storytelling in a non-fiction book is to make the content more relatable, memorable, and accessible to a broader audience.

How you tell the story will determine how your reader feels when reading the book and whether they feel engaged to keep reading or not.

Storytelling is a skill and the best way to master the skill is to follow a framework and practice.

If you remember when you learnt how to drive, in your first lesson you didn't jump into the driver's seat, turn the key in the ignition and drive off at a hundred miles an hour.

It's likely that you started with learning the theory first and learning how to tell your story is no different; we've got to start with the theory and follow a framework.

I first learnt the art of storytelling when I trained in public speaking back in 2019 and the framework to tell your story in a book is extremely similar, known as the Hero's Journey.

The Hero's Journey is made up of three scenes and originated in the theatre during the days of Shakespeare.

I've adapted my application of the Hero's Journey over years of writing many books and storytelling on stages and have summarised it into three scenes:

Scene 1 – The Trigger
Scene 2 – The Test
Scene 3 – The Transformation

Now you might be thinking:

"But Chloë I'm not writing a storybook so why do I need to learn the art of storytelling?"

Well that's probably right, you're not writing your biography or book based on your life story.

But you will be sharing short stories within your chapters as examples to emphasise the process that you're teaching and create a deeper connection to you as the expert.

In all cases, it's still important to engage your reader and grab their attention to want to keep reading, stir their imagination and bring them on the journey with you.

And we do that by following the Hero's Journey:

<u>Scene 1 – The Trigger</u>

The Trigger is the first part of the story and includes the topic, the characters, the setting and most importantly, the incident or activity that set the story in motion known as the "Trigger".

The goal of this scene is for your reader to be bought into the story and be eager to see what happens next.

<u>Scene 2 – The Test</u>

The Test is the part of the story that describes the journey you went on when facing the challenge and how you tried to overcome it.

"Tried" being the key word here because often there are unexpected challenges and problems that unravelled which led to either a longer or more turbulent journey than expected.

This may have left you at a lower point than before and even wondering if there's any point. This is often the longest scene and contains the bulk of the action and suspense.

Scene 3 – The Transformation

The Transformation is the final scene where you share the end results and successes that came from the experience.

It usually involves finding a new path or strategy which leads to the outcome that you wanted. As the final scene in the Hero's Journey, it usually provides a sense of closure and ending.

Let's put the Hero's Journey into context when reading a well-known story:

The Little Mermaid

Scene 1: The Trigger

We're introduced to Ariel, a young mermaid who is fascinated with the human world above the sea.

She longs to experience life on land, but her father, King Triton, forbids it.

This triggers Ariel to make a deal with the sea witch Ursula to trade her voice for legs and a chance to win the heart of Prince Eric.

Scene 2: The Test

Ariel falls in love with Prince Eric, but struggles to communicate with him because she no longer has her voice.

Ursula, who is secretly plotting against Ariel, uses this to her advantage and tries to sabotage their relationship.

Ariel must find a way to defeat Ursula and win Eric's heart, all while navigating the challenges of life on land.

Scene 3: The Transformation

Ariel convinces Eric that Ursula is pretending to be her and Ariel and Eric team up to defeat Ursula.

They battle Ursula and save the kingdom.

Ariel's voice is restored and she finally gets her happily ever after with Eric.

And if you watch the majority of movies or read fiction books, you'll notice they all follow a similar structure because of the impact on the reader or viewer.

Now let's go through how you can use this framework when storytelling in your book.

Firstly, for a non-fiction book that's based on giving your readers a specific outcome, you won't be writing pages and pages of your story.

You can actually cover all three scenes in 200-300 words.

As mentioned in the previous chapter:

Every story has a point and every point has a story

So, you've got to get clear on what point you're teaching and then pick a story that compliments it.

For example, imagine you're writing a book teaching people how to find themselves and unlock their true power:

Chapter Topic: *Values*

Point: *Establish your values based on what's important to you, not to others.*

Story:

<u>Scene 1 – The Trigger</u>

When I was diagnosed with depression, I had no idea what my values were. In fact, I thought "values" were what companies printed on their walls and put on their website. I had no idea that I could have my own personal values, let alone what they actually were.

<u>Scene 2 – The Test</u>

I found myself asking my friends and family what their values were, on the hunt to find mine. As people shared them, I found myself thinking "oh I like that one!" "that sounds like something I'd like to have" as if I was writing a shopping list.

Before I knew it, I'd written my core values and thought I was finished. As I was telling my coach in our next session, she asked a really powerful question: "Why are they important to you?" and my mind went blank.

As I tried to justify each value, I realised that they weren't as important to me as I thought and what I'd done was write words that I thought would be great values but didn't actually align with me. Back to the drawing board I went.

Scene 3 – The Transformation

So instead of listening to everyone around me, I got my journal and wrote a list of all the things that were important to me and I rated them on a scale of 1-10.

Those that were rated at the top of the scale became my core values. Those core values are still as important to me as they were back then and have given me the clarity to make decisions, navigate uncertainty and reconnect with myself time and time again.

This is an example of how you can weave your stories into the chapters of your book to emphasise points in the process.

Just Takeaways:

- **The Power Of Storytelling:** Storytelling serves as a powerful tool for getting your message across, inspiring your reader, and educating them. Sharing stories help to create a deeper connection between you as the expert and your reader.

- **Tell Your Story:** In a non-fiction book, you'll be teaching your readers to achieve a specific outcome so, whilst it's not just about telling about your whole life story, use your personal experiences to serve as examples to emphasise the processes you're teaching.

- **The Art Of Storytelling:** Storytelling is a skill that anyone can learn through practice and by following a structured framework. The more you write and share stories, the more skilled you become at keeping your reader engaged.

- **The Hero's Journey:** The Hero's Journey is a storytelling framework that has been used since Shakespeare. This three scene framework provides a template for creating engaging stories that can be applied to any story you want to tell.

- **Quality Over Quantity:** Your stories within a non-fiction book don't need to be lengthy. You can effectively cover all three Hero's Journey scenes in a concise 200-300 words. Always keep in mind that every point has a story and every story has a point.

Just Start Writing:

Pick one of your personal experiences and answer the following prompts to come up with some ideas for your three scenes:

<u>Scene 1 – The Trigger</u>

- What's the background or context?
- Where were you and who was involved?
- What was the trigger that led to a change?

<u>Scene 2 – The Test</u>

- What did you do next?
- What did you try?
- What did you do that didn't work?
- What were the unexpected challenges and problems (if any)?
- What happened?

Scene 3 – The Transformation

- What was the end result or success?
- What did you do that achieved that result?
- What did you learn?

You can do this activity and follow this format for all of your personal experiences that you'd like to weave into your book.

Book Writing Blueprint™
1
Purpose
2
Promise
3
Plan
4
Personalise
5
Prepare
6
Publish

"The way to get started is to quit talking and begin doing."

- Walt Disney

10

THE NAME THAT GETS YOUR READERS ATTENTION

Words have the ability to influence, shape and impact our thoughts, emotions and behaviours and it's no different with the name of your book.

So, it's not surprising that people can spend a long time contemplating the name of their book to get it right.

A lot of people come up with names for their book using interesting words, intriguing terms and great metaphors.

My first piece of advice is to not do that.

Yes, it can feel really intelligent and smart to do a play on words or come up with a great metaphor but if your potential reader doesn't understand it, they won't buy it.

And here's a harsh truth.

The name of your book won't define whether people read your book or not.

It will define whether they buy it or not.

So, when naming your book, take your writing hat off and put your marketing hat on!

Research suggests that people form a first impression within the first 7 to 17 seconds which means that it all comes down to the title of your book.

Imagine someone is recommending your book to their friend, you want them to say the title (without any other explanation) and you want their friend to be intrigued and to want to know more.

There's a famous phrase in marketing which is "sell them what they want, give them what they need" and this is the main focus when naming your book.

The name of your book will sell them what they want and the content of your book will show them what they need to get it.

There are three key components of a great book title:

1) What they want

If you could describe what your readers want in 5 words or less, what words would you use?

This is what you want your book title to do. Summarise what they want.

And it's not a surprise that this is going to be very similar to your big promise of the book. The name of your book should connect with the big promise.

2) Who they are

What better way to attract your ideal reader than by labelling the book ready for them.

Use labels or language to define your reader in the name of your book which acts like a big sticker on the book that says "this is made for you!"

3) What they'll get

We want to make it simple for our potential readers to buy your book by making it clear in the title what they actually get like "X steps" or "how to" statement.

Let's take a look at some great examples:

"The 7 Habits of Highly Effective People" by Stephen Covey

"Quiet: The Power of Introverts in a World That Can't Stop Talking" by Susan Cain

"The Lean Startup: How Today's Entrepreneurs Use Continuous Innovation to Create Radically Successful Businesses" by Eric Ries

"Good to Great: Why Some Companies Make the Leap...And Others Don't" by Jim Collins

"Tools of Titans: The Tactics, Routines, and Habits of Billionaires, Icons, and World-Class Performers" by Tim Ferriss.

You'll notice that all of these examples have nailed the three key components:

- **What their readers want:** "highly effective", "radically successful businesses" and "make the leap".

- **Who their readers are:** "introverts", "entrepreneurs" and "companies".

- **What they'll get:** "habits", "tools", "tactics" and "how" statements.

You'll also notice with some of these examples, the book names have both a title and a subtitle.

Having a subtitle can be a great way to capture the theme of your book whilst speaking to the reader and helping them see that the book is written for them.

Now here's an extra sprinkle for you to make your book stand out.

Don't be afraid to put your personality or opinions into the name of your book.

I'm sure there are plenty of experts in your industry that could write a similar book to you but none of them could write it like you.

Put your personality into the name of your book to help it stand out even more.

This is exactly what a great friend of mine, Eva Martins, did with her first book.

Eva's first book is about helping women to achieve more, break the glass ceiling and feel liberated from self-imposed limitations, and we published it on 30th September 2020.

As you haven't met Eva, let me paint a picture for you.

Eva is an incredibly successful woman leading transformation in a large pharmaceutical company.

As a strong woman in a highly male dominated industry, Eva has got a lot of fire and a lot of heart which she brings into her coaching business.

With Eva's strong personality, it's not a surprise that her book is called:

"Stop Believing The B.S.!: 7 Steps to Awaken Your Feminine Power"

This title for Eva's book is a perfect example of how to name your book using your personality and opinions whilst also including the aspects we've mentioned above:

"Stop Believing The B.S.!" – Eva's personality
"7 Steps" – What they'll get
"to Awaken Your Feminine Power" – Who they are and what they want

This book title has helped Eva attract countless clients that have similar personalities and values as Eva and helped her grow her coaching business to a whole new level, as well as still having her senior role in the corporate world.

Bonus Hack:

If you're planning on writing a series or if you've already written a book before and this is your next book, make sure the title stands out and is crystal clear on how this book is different from the others.

Is it a different topic?
Does it serve a different type of reader?
Does it fix a different problem?

Ensure that's clear with the name of your book so that your readers know which book they want to read and why.

Just Takeaways:

- **It's All In The Name:** The title of your book is crucial for attracting your ideal reader, as it's the first impression they get. The primary goal of your book title is to make people want to buy it, not necessarily to convey the full content of the book.

- **Use Your Big Promise:** When giving your book a title, connect with the big promise of the book and refer to exactly what your readers want.

- **Call Them Out:** Include reference in the book title to who your ideal reader is. Use labels that your ideal reader would use to describe themselves or associate with.

- **Tell Them What They'll Get:** Now they know what they want and that it's for them, make it clear what your ideal reader will get. Whether it's a number of steps, or "how" statement, make it clear exactly what they'll get in the book.

- **Use Your Personality:** Don't hesitate to infuse your personality and opinions into your book's title to make it stand out and show your unique style and approach. After all, if they like your personality on the book cover they'll probably enjoy the book too.

- **Make Each Book Different:** If you're writing a series or subsequent books, ensure the title clearly conveys how this book is different from the others in terms of topic, target reader, or problem it addresses.

Just Start Writing:

Follow these steps to come up with a few names for your book:

- Write out the big promise for your book and what your reader wants
- Write a list of labels or words that your reader would use to describe themselves such as "coach", "entrepreneur" or "mum"
- Write a list of words or phrases that describe what they'll get in the book such as "how" statements, "7 steps" or the "process"
- Brainstorm different combinations of these words and phrases to create potential book titles and subtitles
- Ask friends, family, or potential readers for their opinions on your potential book titles and subtitles
- Search your chosen book title(s) on Google or online book stores to see if it is already in use, or if it is too similar to another book title.

11

FINISH YOUR BOOK WITHOUT WRITING A WORD

It's time to put your pen to paper and start writing… or is it?

Writing the first draft of your book can feel quite daunting, especially if you're looking at a blank page knowing you need to fill it with 20,000 to 30,000 words.

This is where I notice a lot of people get blocked because they're stuck on the question of "where do I start".

The answer is anywhere.

There is no right or wrong way to start writing your book.

Pick the chapter you have the most ideas for or the chapter you're most inspired to write.

Don't worry too much about making it perfect at this stage.

Just start!

If you love writing and would call yourself a natural writer, then this is your time to shine.

Start writing and I'll see you in Chapter 12.

However, if you're not big on writing or don't find yourself waking up with inspiration to write beautifully with ease, then I've got some great news for you.

You don't actually have to put pen to paper to write a book.

pause for gasps

You can write and publish a book without ever having to write a word.

more gasps

There are lots of different approaches to doing this to get your inspiration and creative juices flowing. The key is finding the approach that works best for you.

Let's go through a few different ways of doing this:

Ghost Writing

Ghost Writing is a concept where you outsource the writing of your book to someone else and you pay them a fee to do the writing for you.

It's still your book and your asset, they're just paid to get the words on paper for you.

This is something that we've done in Inspired By Publishing for some of our clients and they've loved the process.

The way it works is we get lots of information from them, from any videos they've got, online courses and even Zoom sessions with them.

Once we've got all of the information, we write the manuscript and they have a read through it once it's all done.

Obviously, this is just the creation part. Afterwards they can then edit it, change it and update it until they're happy with their manuscript.

The only caveat I have to share is that it still needs to be your content.

I have seen some entrepreneurs that have had ghost writers write their books and they don't even know what's in them.

Then if their readers approach them saying something along the lines of "oh I just loved the process you taught in Chapter 15. It's completely changed my perspective" and the author has no idea what the reader is referring to.

That's a big no no.

My view is that if it's got your name on it, take the time to make sure it's your content, your stories and ultimately, your book!

Artificial Intelligence (AI)

I couldn't publish a book about writing without mentioning AI.

At the time of writing this book, AI has become a very hot topic in the publishing world.

Put simply, you can use AI software to write parts of your book for you.

And that's exactly what I recommend, only *parts* of your book.

You're writing a book sharing your expertise so to show that you're the expert on that topic.

You're not a robot and you want to make sure you have your own flavour throughout the book, and not that of AI.

That said, using AI to generate ideas, research concepts and even write some pieces can be a great way to speed up the writing process.

But use it with caution.

Remember, AI is available to everyone, including your competitors.

If you want to stand out from everyone else, you don't want to write your whole book using AI that everyone else can use, too.

Speak It

Most people struggle to write because the act of putting their pen to paper (or fingers to a keyboard) gives them the opportunity to overthink.

A quicker and easier way is to speak it and then transcribe it.

You can record yourself speaking the content as if you were talking to a client, friend or team member and then use a transcription tool to turn it into writing.

As a speaker, this is one of my favourite ways to write quickly because you can record yourself on the go whenever you get bits of inspiration.

In all three of these options, once you've got the words on the paper, your job is to edit, review and rewrite it to sound more like you.

The risk of using any of these tools to write your book is that it could lose your essence or style as an author and even if you wouldn't call yourself a writer, you still want it to sound like you!

There is no value in being an authority if there is no authenticity.

After all, there is nothing worse than reading a book, feeling like you've really gotten to know the author and then seeing the author on social media or on stage and realise they're completely different to the person in the book.

And with AI, readers are more sceptical than ever.

So when putting your pen to paper, here are some key do's and don'ts:

DON'T try to be someone that you're not!

I know that writing a book can be a scary thing to do and often we feel like we're opening ourselves up to criticism so it can feel easier to try and act like someone else.

But resist the urge to hide or change who you are and just be yourself! By being yourself, you'll attract people that resonate with you and they'll be more likely to stay connected to find out more.

DON'T change how you write or try to sound more "professional"!

Many entrepreneurs use apps like thesauraus.com and the synonyms features in writing tools to be able to come up with innovative and intelligent ways of describing what they mean.

Whilst you'll sound incredibly smart doing this, it's the quickest way to alienate your audience because it's not you and therefore it's unlikely to be what your audience connect with either.

I recommend writing how you speak.

If you're known for using certain words then use them in your book. If you're known for swearing or cursing, then go for it!

DO allow yourself to be vulnerable

People buy from who they know, like and trust – right?

Well a great way to build trust is to be vulnerable with your readers. Show them that you're human and share some of the not so glamourous parts of you and your story.

This will help your readers to relate to you whilst also managing their expectations.

For example, if you're not a strong writer, tell your readers!

Include it in the introduction as part of why you're writing the book and not only will it help them to trust you earlier in the process, it will also help to take some of the pressure off you to make it perfect.

DO write in your normal tone of voice

When someone reads a book, they are hearing a voice in their heads reading the words out loud, this is known as "subvocalisation".

With a physical book, the only way to get your message across in the way you'd normally say it is with the tone of voice so that they can read it in their heads in the same way you would say it.

If you're normally quite authoritative and assertive, then use that tone of voice in your writing.

If you're normally quite friendly and witty, making jokes or adding humour into how you speak, use that tone of voice in your writing.

For example, you can probably tell by this point in the book that I prefer to write in a conversational tone of voice with a hint of humour now and then.

This is because I'm a speaker and I love to entertain audiences when I'm sharing my knowledge with them.

So, when writing this book, it's important to me to ensure that it comes across in the words and language I use so that you can get an idea of my personality, in the same way your readers will with your book.

Just Takeaways:

- **Just Start Writing:** Writing the first draft of your book may seem daunting so the key to avoiding overwhelm is to start writing anywhere; there's no right or wrong way to get started.

- **Perfection Can Wait:** Your writing doesn't need to be perfect in the initial stages, the most important thing is to start. There's plenty of time to put your perfectionist hat back on later in the publishing process.

- **Ghost Writing:** Ghost writing involves outsourcing your book's writing to someone else who gets paid to write for you. It's still your book that you own but you need to ensure the content truly reflects your ideas and voice.

- **Artificial Intelligence (AI)**: AI can help with brainstorming ideas, researching concepts, and even writing parts of your book, but use it sparingly. Don't rely solely on using AI, as it can leave you sounding like a robot and not like you!

- **Speaking Your Book:** Recording yourself speaking the content and then transcribing it is a faster and easier way to write. This method allows you to capture inspiration on the go.

- **It's All In The Edit:** Whichever method you use, you have the words on paper, your job is to edit and review it to make sure you're happy with it and that it feels and sounds like you.

- **Be Yourself:** When writing your book, be yourself and don't try to be someone you're not. Write in your normal tone of voice, just like how you'd speak to your reader in person and let your personality and tone shine through in your writing!

- **Be Honest And Vulnerable:** Allow yourself to be vulnerable and share the less glamorous parts of your story. This will help your readers to relate to you and trust you whilst also managing their expectations of what the journey is like.

Just Start Writing:

Consider the different ways to write or speak your book and which way appeals to you the most.

Pick a chapter that you're most interested in or motivated to start with and try using a ghost writer, AI or speaking your book and transcribing it.

Review what's been written and practice editing it.

Use this activity to find your preferred method and rinse and repeat!

12

THE #1 SECRET TO GET IT DONE FAST

Many entrepreneurs ask me:

"How can I finish writing my book as quickly as possible?"

And my response is always the same:

"How consistent can you be with writing it?"

Before I explain what I mean by that, let's look at it from a different angle.

What stops people from writing their book?

What slows them down?

They lose momentum, also known as “writer's block”, and the reason they lose momentum is because they stop writing.

We’re all pretty busy people and when we start a big project like writing a book, something can easily get in the way if we let it.

We get distracted, life takes over and a day has turned into a week and, before you know it, a whole month has passed since you last opened that word document and wrote something.

And whilst time has been passing by, your guilt of letting all of the time pass has made the thought of writing again to be way more effort and feel like so much more hard work.

Time + Guilt + Effort = One Unfinished Book

So, what’s the best way to not lose momentum?

Don’t stop writing.

Be consistent and create a habit of writing something <u>every day</u>.

It could be 100 words, it could be 1000 words – the volume isn't as important as the habit you're creating.

The act of doing some writing every day not only helps you write it quicker but it feels like less work because it's been broken down into smaller chunks.

That's how you can avoid falling into the trap of taking years to write a book that could've been finished in just a few months, by creating a habit to write something every day.

When I wrote my first book, I found this quite challenging because my schedule was already pretty hectic and I'm an all-or-nothing kinda girl.

The idea of booking a week off, flying to a sunny destination and writing my book in peace and quiet was extremely tempting but just not feasible at all.

I knew that if I was going to wait until I had a completely clear few weeks to focus on only writing my book, I would have been waiting for a while!

I decided to set aside 30 minutes every morning to write something.

The first few days were fairly difficult, racking my brain to try and get something down so I could move onto the rest of my busy day.

But later that week I found myself in flow and the 30 minutes of writing turned into 60 minutes and even 2 hours on some days where I could squeeze it in.

It was like a tap that had started running and I didn't want to turn it off. The inspiration came and the words kept flowing, consistently every day.

And on the odd days where I didn't feel like writing, I spent the time researching ideas for the chapter and quickly the words started flowing again.

I'd set myself a goal of writing my book in a month and people thought I was crazy. Yet writing consistently everyday meant that I'd finished the first draft of the manuscript in just 10 days!

And let me be clear, I am not a writer.

Back then I wasn't even in the publishing industry.

I just followed the process and stayed consistent until it was done.

The journey of a thousand miles starts with one step. The journey of a thousand words starts with one letter.

I've now taught this process to hundreds of entrepreneurs with incredibly busy schedules including a friend of mine, Rosalia Lazzara-Tilley.

Rosalia came to me in April 2023 as she wanted help with finishing her book.

She had written some content and knew the topic of the book but couldn't get into the flow of writing it and get it done.

Rosalia has a very successful marketing agency that specialises in helping mortgage brokers to build their online presence and get leads from social media and as she's always creating content for her clients, Rosalia didn't have much spare time to write her own content for her book.

We started working on Rosalia's book in May 2023 and despite her extremely busy schedule, we set her a target of writing a chapter a week and Rosalia and I had weekly 1:1 sessions for accountability.

Within 8 weeks Rosalia had written all of her chapters and we started the publishing process.

Rosalia's book "Social Media Guide for Mortgage Brokers" launched on 17th October 2023 and hit number 1 on Amazon in six categories as a bestseller in less than 12 hours. Since talking about her book, Rosalia's been invited to speak on stages and on podcasts to share her message to other financial professionals.

This never would have been possible if it wasn't for her commitment to the schedule and accountability that we put in place to get her book finished.

So, if you want to write your book quickly, set aside time every day to write something and create the habit.

You may not hit it off straight away but once you get started, you'll find the momentum and just keep writing.

The best motivator is results and once you see your word count going up and up each day, it's the best motivator to keep writing.

Dedicated Time + Consistency + Motivation = One Finished Book!

Just Takeaways:

- **The Formula For Writing Fast:** The key to writing a book quickly is to schedule dedicated writing time, be consistent and stay motivated.

- **Be Consistent:** Most authors get stuck with writer's block because they stop writing and lose momentum. The key to finishing your book quickly is consistency in your writing routine.

- **Write Everyday:** Consistently write something every day, even if it's a small amount, to create a habit and maintain your flow. Consistent, daily writing breaks the process into smaller, manageable chunks, making it feel less overwhelming.

- **There's Never A "Perfect" Time:** Don't wait for the perfect time or ideal conditions to write, as it may never come. Waiting for a clear schedule can lead to the book remaining unfinished for a long time.

- **What Gets Scheduled Gets Done:** Allocate a specific time each day for writing, even if it's just 30 minutes. Starting may be difficult at first, but as you establish the habit, you'll find it easier to write more and stay in the flow.

- **Surprise Yourself:** Consistency can lead to unexpected progress; a tap of inspiration may open, and you'll write more than you expect. Seeing your word count increase daily serves as a powerful motivator to keep writing and finish your book.

Just Start Writing:

Open your calendar on your phone or computer and block out time to do 30 minutes on your book each day.

Where possible stick to the same time of day so you can build the habit easier.

Make sure that everyone who can access your calendar or may need to contact you, like team members or family members, know what this time is for and the importance of it being uninterrupted.

You'll thank me later!

13

DESIGN A COVER THAT SELLS

"Don't judge a book by its cover" is one of the most common phrases when describing first impressions. That said, people *will* judge your book by its cover and the way it looks.

We know that people form a first impression within the first 7 to 17 seconds. Well studies have also shown that up to 90% of initial judgments are based on colour and design.

That means that we have 7 seconds to attract our readers and 90% of that will come from the design of the book cover.

No pressure.

Your book cover is the wrapping paper of your book, it's the casing that will attract your reader to pick it up in a bookstore or click on it online to find out what it's about.

A lot of people I come across want to design their book cover earlier in the process and you might have been reading this book thinking the same thing.

But given that we only have 7 seconds to grab their attention, you don't want to waste it by not wholly capturing the true essence of your book.

Designing your book cover after your book is finished means you can properly capture everything throughout the elements of the cover.

Here are a few tips when designing your book cover:

1) Step into your readers shoes

By now you'll know your ideal reader pretty well. So what do you think will attract them?

If they've craving calm and your book is going to help them with that, then design a cover that helps them feel calm, relaxed and stress-free.

If they're bored and want to strive for more, then design a cover that gives them that feeling.

Always focus on how you want your reader to feel when looking at the cover and run with that.

2) Look at what others are doing

Use your research from Chapter 2 to look at covers of other books similar to yours.

- What do you like?
- What do you dislike?
- What are the similarities?
- What stands out?

Just because others are doing something doesn't mean you should be doing it too but it's good to see what else is out there in your industry and if there are any features that align with you.

3) Establish a book brand

People crave certainty and consistency, so meet their needs by creating a consistent book brand.

This could be in line with your personal or business brand or it could be a slight variation.

Think fonts, colours, shapes, images or illustrations that symbolise you, your brand and what your book is all about.

By creating a book brand not only does it help your readers remember you, it also helps to make your mark amongst your competitors and help your book stand out!

4) Use your face wisely

As we know, your book is not about you but you are the author and so your face needs to be on it somewhere.

Some entrepreneurs like their face to be on the cover, others prefer to not have their face anywhere.

I recommend a middle ground by putting your face on the back of your book along with your bio.

This lets the reader see you and feel like they know you without the book feeling that it's about you and you alone.

5) Go professional or go home

Now I know this might be hard to hear but your cover needs to be designed by a professional.

This could well be you if you are a graphic designer or creative, fantastic! But if not, don't try to do it yourself. The last thing you want is to spend months or even years working on the content in your book and never get any readers because the cover doesn't look professional enough.

Remember, people will judge the contents of your book solely on the cover so if it's not your expertise, hire a professional graphic designer to create the cover for you.

If you plan on working with a publisher, they will be able to do this for you too.

Just Takeaways:

- **First Impression:** First impressions are formed within 7 to 17 seconds, and up to 90% of initial judgments are based on colour and design so your book cover will be the deciding factor whether your ideal reader picks it up, clicks on it or not.

- **Step into Your Reader's Shoes:** When planning your book cover, consider your ideal reader and what will attract them. Plan a cover that will connect with the feelings you want your reader to experience.

- **Look at What Others Are Doing:** Research covers of books similar to yours and have a look at what you like and dislike, commonalities, and key features. You can then choose to model them or go for something completely different.

- **Establish a Book Brand:** Create a consistent book brand that aligns with your personal or business brand. Think about fonts, colours, shapes, and images that represent your book and brand. Consistency helps readers remember you and makes your book stand out in the market.

- **Use Your Face Wisely:** While the book is not about you, as the author, it's a good idea to include your face somewhere on the cover. The best place is to include your face on the back cover along with your bio to create a connection with readers without making it about you alone.

- **Go Professional or Go Home:** It's vital that your book cover is designed by a professional so you give your reader a professional first impression. You can hire a graphic designer or if you're working with a publisher, they'll do the cover design too.

Just Start Writing:

Follow the five steps and make notes on your initial ideas for your book cover including:

- Colours
- Shapes
- Fonts
- Styles
- Images
- Layouts

And anything else that stands out to you!

Let your imagination run wild and see what you can come up with.

6
Publish
1
Purpose
5
Prepare
Book Writing
Blueprint™
2
Promise
4
Personalise
3
Plan

"The last 10% it takes to a launch something takes as much energy as the first 90%"

- Rob Kalin

14

THE GOOD, THE BAD & THE UGLY

It's time to talk about publishing!

At this point you might be half way through writing your book, maybe you've even finished it and wondering how you can get it out to the world.

Or you might still be writing and just being curious to find out more about the publishing process so you can be prepared for what's coming up next.

Well you'll be glad to know that in this chapter I'm going to run you through the different routes of publishing and how to work out which route is best for you.

Deciding how to publish your book is vital to ensuring your book gets into the hands of the people that you want to help.

The reality is, so many books get written and don't actually get published and there are three common reasons why:

Reason 1: The author doesn't have the knowledge on how to publish their book

Reason 2: The author doesn't have the contacts to get their book out there

Reason 3: The author gets in their own way, procrastinates or delays and never actually publishes their book.

The sad thing is that you can have the most valuable, well-written book in the world but if you let any of these reasons get in the way, your book can end up being the world's best kept secret and never actually inspire the people that it's written for.

There are three methods of publishing your book:

- Traditional publishing
- Self-publishing; and
- Hybrid publishing

Traditional Publishing

In the past this was the most common method of publishing books by working with publishing houses like Hay House, Penguin and many other big names.

I call it "traditional publishing" because for many years, it was the only avenue for publishing books and required entrepreneurs to submit a pitch about their book, and publishing houses would either say yes or no.

If you were lucky to get a yes from a publishing house, then the publishing house would take everything off your hands from editing, design, distribution, marketing and of course, sales.

They ensure your book is distributed to all of their contacts and all of the bookstores in their black book.

But where there is a significant result there is also an equally significant cost with traditional publishing taking a significantly large percentage of your book sales.

This percentage can be as much as 85%-95% leaving you with only 5%-15% of the money made from your book sales.

Now some people often say that it's better to get 5% of something than 100% of nothing and to some extent I'd agree with that.

But what if you want to give your book away for free and you have to buy the books from your traditional publisher?

Or if you want to change something in your book or turn it into an online course and the traditional publisher doesn't give you permission?

Traditional publishers often keep the rights of your book so that they get a cut if your book is turned into other revenue generating items like an audiobook, movie or other products or merchandise.

When I wrote "Determined and Dangerous" back in 2019 I spent a considerable amount of time considering whether to pitch my book to traditional publishers and I made the decision not to.

I knew that working with a publishing house would have been incredible for my brand and my business, but I knew I wanted to have freedom to write how I wanted to and have full control to earn from it and use my book without needing to ask permission from others, so I decided to try the self-publishing route.

Self-Publishing

This is where you work independently from publishers and you decide to publish your book yourself.

This method is still fairly new and only really became popular in the early 2000s when online platforms were launched that provide entrepreneurs with a direct way to publish and distribute their books worldwide.

The most common self-publishing platform is Kindle Direct Publishing, part of the Amazon group, which was launched in 2007 and introduced entrepreneurs to "print-on-demand" where your book is only printed when it's sold so you don't need to order thousands of copies of your book to publish it.

I absolutely fell in love with the idea of self-publishing because it meant that I had complete independence in my publishing journey and had free reign to do it the way I really wanted to.

It also meant that I had no upfront printing cost and I could get 100% of the profits.

The reality though, wasn't quite as freeing as it sounds because, without a publisher, the authors are then responsible for everything.

That means you are responsible for the editing, design, distribution, marketing and sales of the book, as well as actually writing it!

And for many authors, this can mean it takes a lot more time and effort to learn how to do it and who you need around you to make it happen.

It can also feel like a very lonely journey without an experienced team to bounce your ideas off and discuss strategies.

This is where I see a lot of entrepreneurs writing great books and never actually publishing them because they're overwhelmed with the publishing, marketing and sales processes.

Hybrid Publishing

This is the newest of the publishing methods and is a middle ground between traditional publishing and self-publishing.

Hybrid publishing is where you have a publishing agency to publish your book and take the stress out of the publishing process without taking ownership of the book or a percentage of your sales.

Similar to traditional publishing, hybrid publishers are listed in your book as your publisher and so they're motivated to market your book and get sales for you because they want to showcase their brand, making it a win-win.

Now before you think it sounds too good to be true, I need to be clear that hybrid publishing agencies do charge for their services but it's typically a fixed fee rather than a percentage of all of your book sales making it a lot more cost effective for authors.

Hybrid publishing is similar to the self-publishing route where you can print-on-demand but a key difference is that hybrid publishers can get your book published on multiple platforms in many different formats, expanding your reach rather than being on one self-publishing platform.

This method of publishing has completely changed the publishing industry and it's one of the reasons why I started Inspired By Publishing.

Picking your publisher

Now if you've decided that you want to work with a publisher, whether a traditional publisher or hybrid publisher, it can be quite overwhelming comparing and deciding who to work with.

Here are a couple of key considerations to think about:

1. What other books have they published? Do they have experience in your industry and with your ideal readers?

2. How flexible are they with your content? Do they have tight word counts, page numbers or limits on images?

3. What book formats do they publish? Do they specialise in one format or can they publish in different formats?

4. Where do they publish books? Do they publish on only one platform or multiple different bookstores?

5. What are their marketing strategies? How do they get your book out there?

6. How do they measure success? How will they determine if your book has done well or not?

7. How long does it take to publish? Do they have a proven process to bring your book to market?

8. How flexible is their timeline? Do they have strict deadlines and expiry dates or can they be flexible around your schedule?

9. How do they involve you in the process? Do they have regular meetings or touch points with you to keep you updated?

Bonus Hack:

When speaking to publishers, ask them:

"What is it that you don't do that I need to do?"

This will help you to ensure you're both on the same page and know if there are any gaps in their services.

Just Takeaways:

- **Get Published:** Many well-written books remain unpublished due to three common reasons: lack of publishing knowledge, limited publishing contacts, and self-sabotage through procrastination. Don't fall into any of these traps!

- **Publishing Methods:** Choosing the right publishing method is essential for reaching your target audience effectively and avoiding common pitfalls. There are three methods for publishing your book which are traditional publishing, self-publishing and hybrid publishing.

- **Traditional Publishing:** The most common of the publishing methods involves working with established publishing houses that publish your book for a substantial cut of your book sales. Whilst using a well-known publishing house will help you get your book out to the masses, it often means you'll need their approval to use your book for other purposes like repurposing or giving free copies.

- **Self-Publishing:** Launched in the early 2000s with platforms like Kindle Direct Publishing (Amazon), self-publishing offers complete independence for authors to publish their books with no upfront printing costs. However, authors must handle all aspects of publishing, including editing, design, distribution, marketing, and sales, which can be overwhelming without a support team.

- **Hybrid Publishing:** A blended approach where a publishing agency assists in publishing your book on multiple platforms and in various formats, increasing the book's reach without taking ownership of the book or a percentage of sales. Hybrid publishers charge fixed fee to manage the publishing, marketing and promotion of your book making it the most cost-effective.

- **Selecting Your Publisher:** When choosing a publisher, consider factors like their experience in your industry, flexibility with content, book formats, distribution platforms, marketing strategies and timeline for publication. Ask them how they measure success and their involvement in the publishing process to ensure your objectives are aligned.

Just Start Writing:

Write your own pros and cons list for each publishing method.

If you choose to use a hybrid publisher or traditional publisher, take action and contact them to find out how they can support you with getting your book out there.

There's no better form of accountability to finish your book than having committed to publisher who will keep you going!

15

BOOK SIZE DOES MATTER

If you're reading this chapter then it's likely you've either finished writing your book or are close to finishing and now you're probably wondering about more of the practical aspects of publishing your book.

There are 20+ formats for publishing books but for ease, here are the most commonly published formats:

Paperback

These are arguably the most popular printed books which have flexible paper covers. They're cost effective, compact and portable hence why they're the most popular among readers.

Hardback

Also known as hardcover, these books have a rigid cover made of cardboard and are usually more durable than paperback books.

As such, they are more expensive to print and typically used for higher priced books or special editions.

E-book

E-books or electronic books are digital versions of print books that can be read on e-readers, tablets, smartphones, and computers. These are also commonly known as kindle books.

Audiobook

These are audio recordings of books that allow people to listen to the content instead of reading it. They can be bought, downloaded or streamed from most online book stores including Audible, Spotify and Apple Books.

In an ideal world you'd publish your book in all four formats to serve different types of readers and meet the majority of their needs, but we've all got to start somewhere.

Now when it comes to publishing a book, size does matter!

But I don't mean the word count or number of chapters in your book, I'm referring to the size of your book when it's printed.

This is the physical height, length and width of your book.

Similar to what we've mentioned previously, first impressions count and people will make assumptions about the value of the content in your book by the size of the book and how it feels when they pick it up.

Does it look too small to be valuable?

Does it look too thin to have enough information in it?

This doesn't mean small or thin books are bad, it just means those sizes are used for books that want to be seen as "easy reads", "quick guides" or "pocket books" for example.

Does it look too thick and too much to read?

Does it look too big to carry and read on the go?

This also doesn't mean big or thick books are bad either, in the same way it just means that those larger books are usually great for education or in-depth books for example.

So before we go into printing sizes, get clear on how you want your book to be packaged.

Do you want it to be a quick pocket-sized guide?

Do you want your readers to read it on the go?

Do you want your readers to feel it's high value and packed with information?

Do you want your readers to sit down and concentrate as they read it?

These considerations will help you to decide the size and weight of your book.

Here are the most common sizes for different types of printed books:

- Self-Help and How-To Books are typically printed as 5.5" x 8.5" and the page counts range from 150 to 300 pages. Shorter books are not uncommon if the content is concise and focused though.

- Business and Personal Development books are similar to self-help books and are usually either 5.5" x 8.5" and 6" x 9" with a range from 150 to 300 pages.

- Travel Guides or Cookbooks vary based on the amount of information provided but are typically 7" x 10" in size with 100 to 300 pages.

- Biographies are probably the most varied and can depend on the scope and depth of personal experiences shared. They're usually 6" x 9" in size and usually from 200 to 500 in pages.

Of course, there are no hard or strict rules on the size of your book or the number of words though.

I've shared the examples with you above to use as a guide to help you on your publishing journey but feel free to deviate and go with what feels right for your book.

Just Takeaways:

- **Book Formats:** There are 20+ formats that you can publish your book in but the most commonly used are paperback, hardback, e-book (or kindle) and audiobook.

- **Publishing in Multiple Formats:** In an ideal world, publishing your book in multiple formats caters to different reader preferences but don't let it overwhelm you. Start with paperback and then scale from there.

- **Size Matters:** Size refers to the physical dimensions of your book: height, length, and width. Readers often judge the value of a book by its size and feel. Smaller books are seen as "easy reads" or "pocket books" whereas larger books are suitable for education or in-depth content.

- **Determine Your Book's Use:** Decide whether you want your book to be a quick pocket-sized guide, suitable for on-the-go reading, high in value, or for concentrated reading. Your choice will influence the size and weight of your book.

- **Common Book Sizes:** The most common sizes for a non-fiction book are 5.5" x 8.5" or 6" x 9" with 150 to 300 pages. This may vary for the type of book where travel guides are typically smaller and cookbooks are typically bigger.

- **No Strict Rules:** While there are common sizes for different book types, there are no strict rules regarding book size or page count. You can use the examples as a guide, but feel free to choose the size that best suits your book's content and purpose.

Just Start Writing:

Go back to your research in Chapter 2 and take a look at the similar books in your industry.

You can usually find this in the information section if you're looking at an online book store.

What formats is the book available in?

What size is the book?

What's the page count?

What assumptions could you make about those books based on the size and page count?

By doing this research you can compare others in your industry and decide if you want to be similar or go for a different angle.

16

MARKETING MISTAKES TO AVOID

Congratulations! You've come to the end of the Book Writing Blueprint™ and now have everything you need to write and publish your book.

But publishing your book only makes your book available, it doesn't necessarily mean readers and sales. That all comes from promoting your book.

So, whilst this book isn't designed to teach you how to market your book, I'm going to finish with some tips on promoting your book so you can get your book into the hands of the people that need it.

Through Inspired By Publishing I've met hundreds of entrepreneurs who have published their books but come to us to ask if we can relaunch them because they didn't get many sales the first time they tried.

Please don't make this same mistake.

The reason many entrepreneurs don't make many book sales is because of their approach to marketing and promoting their books.

People buy from people they know, like and trust and buying a book is no different.

Now when you first publish your book, the first people that will buy it will likely be people that know you, like you and trust you so where do people go wrong?

Well it's not that potential readers don't know, like or trust you, it's that they don't know, like or trust your book yet!

Many people write their books, publish them, close their eyes, cross their fingers and hope that people buy. It might come as a surprise but very rarely does that work!

If people don't know that your book exists, obviously they're not going to buy it.

So, what you want to be thinking about at this stage is <u>not:</u>

How can I help potential readers to know, like and trust me?

But instead:

How can I help potential readers to know the book?

How can I help potential readers to like the book?

How can I help potential readers to trust the book?

And this needs to be the focus of your marketing for your book.

Here are a few tips to put this into practice:

Early bird catches the worm

Talk about your book as early in the process as possible. Tell people that you're writing a book, post about it on social media and ask for their advice where you can.

The sooner they know about the book, the sooner they join you on the journey and support you.

Share small extracts, tips and sneak peeks

The best way to encourage people to like your book is to share sneak peeks and extracts from the book to give them a taste of what to expect.

This can be on social media, webinars, podcasts or anywhere you can share your message.

If they're your ideal reader they'll like the content and stay tuned to get their copy of your book when they can.

Openly share your story

Trust is built through vulnerability and transparency so, to help your potential readers trust your book, share stories with them that show your vulnerability.

We've been through the 5Fs in Chapter 8 so share some of these in your marketing and reassure your potential readers that you understand the problems they're facing right now.

Tell them when and how to buy it

Sometimes we need to be spoon fed and people like us to make it easy for them! Set a date that your book will be available, tell them how and where they can purchase it and give them clear instructions.

When it's available to buy, give them the link and a reason to buy it now.

Whether it's a launch offer or exclusive bonuses, make it a no brainer for them to get their copy.

Here's a great example of an effective marketing strategy for a book for you to model.

Jasmin Manke's "Co-Creating Abundance: Attracting Wealth With Ease" launched on 22nd February 2022. (For anyone like me that loves numerology, 22/2/2022 is not a bad launch date!)

As soon as we started working on Jasmin's book she was talking about it on her social media, on her stories, on stages and at events so everyone knew about it.

In fact, she documented most of the journey, including selfies of her writing the book, screenshots of when we first showed her the digital cover and even doing Instagram 'lives' when she got her first proof copy in her hands. This is what she shared with everyone.

As we were about to send her book to print, Jasmin found out that she'd been named on the Forbes 30 under 30 list, a huge achievement.

Luckily it was just in time for us to add that to her book cover!

This is the power of marketing your book before it's available.

It's not just about the additional book sales but the additional visibility and press opportunities that it can bring. You never know who is watching!

It doesn't need to be perfectly designed social media graphics or professionally written email campaigns, some of the most shared and engaged content is when it's you and your phone taking people on the journey with you.

In summary, when marketing your book, your goal is to unapologetically shout about it from the rooftops and get other people to shout with you.

Ok, shouting from the rooftops might seem a bit daunting, that's just my energy, but for you it could be talking about it softly to people or making sarcastic jokes about it.

The tone isn't as important as the purpose; to unapologetically tell people about it and encourage others to talk about it too.

Bring your readers on the journey with you. The end of your journey is the beginning of theirs.

Just Takeaways:

- **Publishing Vs Promotion:** Many entrepreneurs fail to get book sales due to not effectively promoting their book. Publishing your book is just the first step; promoting it is key for readers and sales.

- **Build Trust With Your Book:** People buy from those they know, like, and trust. Your potential readers may already know, like and trust you but they also need to know, like and trust your book.

- **Early Bird Catches The Worm:** Start talking about your book early in the publishing process. Share your book-writing journey on social media and seek advice. The sooner people know about your book, the more support you'll gain when you launch it.

- **Give Them A Sneak Peak:** Provide sneak peeks and extracts to give readers a taste of your book and get them excited. Share content on social media, webinars, podcasts, or any available platform. Be proactive and enthusiastic about sharing your book with the world!

- **Tell Them When And How to Buy It:** When your book has launched, make sure you provide clear instructions on when, where, and how to purchase your book and make it really easy by giving a direct link.

- **Sweeten The Deal:** People will already want to support you in launching your book but make it a no brainer by giving them a compelling reason through discounts or exclusive bonuses if they are the first to get their copy.

- **Unapologetically Promote Your Book:** Your goal in marketing your book is to promote it unapologetically and encourage others to do the same. You can promote it in your own unique way, whether loudly or subtly, as long as the purpose is to get people talking about it.

Just Start Writing:

Post on your social media telling people about your book.

It could be asking them to vote on the book name or sharing a sneak peek of the book cover and asking for their feedback.

You could even be bold and announce that you've set yourself the challenge of writing your own book and give them an insight as to what it will be about.

Post it on your social media and start marketing your soon-to-be published book!

CONCLUSION

Deciding to write and publish your own book is a significant step towards establishing yourself as an authority in your industry.

Throughout this book, I've taken you through the Book Writing Blueprint™, our six-step process that takes you from the inception of your book idea to its publication and beyond.

We've touched upon the importance of having a clear purpose, defining your target audience, planning your book, understanding your process, infusing it with your personal stories, and overcoming the challenges of preparing and publishing your book.

The power of a published book goes far beyond the pages; it elevates you into a recognised expert, someone whose words hold weight and inspire others.

There might be a part of you that feels like writing a book is like hiking up a mountain and it still might feel like a lot of work.

But the best part is that you've now got the steps to follow to get you to the top of that mountain and beyond.

With a well-structured plan in place, you'll always know where to begin and where to go next.

I've intentionally written this book to provide you with guidance on outlining your book and determining what content to include so you never get lost in the process and with short chapters so you can easily go back if you need to recap.

Especially if, like many entrepreneurs, you wouldn't call yourself a "writer" or "author".

Let's be honest, the concept of writing and publishing your book can lead to all kinds of challenges including writer's block, procrastination and perfectionism and I'm hoping by reading this book you've learnt how to overcome each of these challenges and more.

But remember, you don't want to have the best book that never gets published or read.

Set yourself up for success with the right resources, time and people to publish, distribute and promote your book.

Your book has the potential to impact lives, but it must reach the people who need it to make that happen.

So, if you're serious about making your mark in your industry, if you want to inspire others, share your expertise, and build a lasting legacy, then make sure you've got everything you need to make it a success.

If you haven't already, get access to the additional resources to compliment the content in this book at www.chloebisson.com/justwrite and learn more about how Inspired By Publishing can support you in turning your book-publishing dreams into a reality.

Remember, the journey of a thousand words begins with a single letter!

So here is your last kick up the arse to start today, transform your ideas into a powerful book that will leave a lasting impact and get published!

ABOUT THE AUTHOR

Chloë Bisson is a publishing and storytelling expert, host of the Inspired By show, a #1 bestselling author, international speaker and multi-award winning entrepreneur.

As a chartered accountant at the age of 21 and director by the age of 24, Chloë's success came to a sharp halt when she was diagnosed with severe clinical depression at the age of 25.

After months of growth and recovery, Chloë knew she was meant for more than just the normal path and began her journey of entrepreneurship.

Since then she's been featured on the cover of Global Woman magazine, spoken on stage internationally and been featured on BBC, Fox, ABC, NBC, CW, London Business Magazine, Business Woman Today, Foundr, COACH Magazine and Thrive Global.

Today, Chloë runs Inspired By Publishing; a book publishing agency that helps entrepreneurs to write and publish their books so that they can share their expertise, tell their story and be seen as the authority that they are.

REFERENCES

Alexander's. (n.d.). Historical Printing Facts. Alexander's Print Advantage. Retrieved from https://alexanders.com/blog/surprising-world-printing-facts/

Bisson, C. (2019). Determined and Dangerous. Independently Published.

Martins, C. (2022). How Do You Survive When Mum and Dad Separate?. Independently Published.

Covey, S. R. (2020). The 7 Habits of Highly Effective People: 30th Anniversary Edition (The Covey Habits). Simon & Schuster.

Dhunna, A. (2022). How To Win Customers With Google Ads. Independently Published.

Skyler Fontana.com. Origins of Hero's Journey and Three Act Structure. Alexander's Print SkylerFontana.com. Retrieved from https://skylerfontana.com/origins-hero-journey-three-acts/

The Little Mermaid. (1989). Directed by Ron Clements and John Musker. [Film]. Walt Disney Pictures.

Cain, S. (2013). Quiet: The Power of Introverts in a World That Can't Stop Talking. Penguin.

Ries, E. (2011). The Lean Startup: How Today's Entrepreneurs Use Continuous Innovation to Create Radically Successful Businesses. Portfolio Penguin.

Collins, J. C. (1975). Good to Great: Why Some Companies Make the Leap...And Others Don't. Random House Business.

Ferriss, T. (2016). Tools of Titans: The Tactics, Routines, and Habits of Billionaires, Icons, and World-Class Performers. Vermilion.

Martins, E. (2020). Stop Believing The B.S.!: 7 Steps to Awaken Your Feminine Power. Independently Published.

Lazzara, R. (2023). Social Media Guide for Mortgage Brokers. Inspired By Publishing.

Amazon Staff. (2017). A look back at 10 years of the Amazon Kindle. Amazon.com, Inc. Retrieved from https://www.aboutamazon.com/news/devices/a-look-back-at-10-years-of-the-amazon-kindle

Manke, J. (2022). Co-Creating Abundance: Attracting Wealth With Ease. Independently Published.

Printed in Dunstable, United Kingdom

77031354R00127